D1433388

The Economist

Pocket Guide to Marketing

Related titles in this series:

The Pocket Economist
Rupert Pennant-Rea and Bill Emmott

The Economist Pocket Accountant
Christopher Nobes

The Economist Pocket Banker
Tim Hindle

The Economist Pocket Guide to Defence
Michael Sheehan and James Wyllie

The Economist

Pocket Guide to
Marketing

Michael Thomas

Basil Blackwell

and

The Economist

Jointly published 1986
Basil Blackwell Ltd
108 Cowley Road, Oxford OX4 1JF, UK
and The Economist
Publications Ltd
40 Duke Street
London W1A 1DW

Basil Blackwell Inc.
432 Park Avenue South, Suite 1503
New York, NY 10016, USA

British Library Cataloguing in Publication Data
Thomas, Michael, *1933 July 15-*
    The economist pocket guide to marketing
    1. Marketing—Dictionaries
    I. Title
    658.8′003′21   HF5412

    ISBN 0-631-14767-5

Library of Congress Cataloging in Publication Data
Thomas, Michael, 1933-
    The Economist pocket guide to marketing.

    1. Marketing—Dictionaries. I. Title.
    II. Title: Pocket guide to marketing.
    HF5415.T4978   1986   658.8′003   86-8242
    ISBN 0-631-14767-5

Typeset by Katerprint Typesetting Services Ltd, Oxford
Printed in Great Britain by Billing and Sons Ltd, Worcester

Contents

Consumption is the sole end and purpose of all production; and the interest of the producer ought to be attended to, only so far as it may be necessary for promoting that of the consumer.

Adam Smith

Companies . . . recognize that the marketplace, not the factory, ultimately determines which firms will succeed. Their challenge is to find ways to reconcile company profitability, customer-need satisfaction and social responsibility.

Professor Philip Kotler

Marketing is merely a civilized form of warfare in which most battles are won with words, ideas and disciplined thinking.

Albert W. Emery

Preface

Because we are all consumers, and have been active buyers ever since we purchased our first sweets/candy, we all think we know a great deal about marketing. Few consumers, however, see beyond the immediate shopping experience to the complex processes that bring them the goods and services they buy.

Contrary to some popular opinion, marketing is not advertising, nor is it selling. The real world of marketing is about products, product development, product differentiation, and product distribution. Above all it is about finding and satisfying customers.

The *Pocket Guide to Marketing* tries to provide a window from which to view and understand some of the complex processes of marketing.

I could not have prepared the manuscript without the help of my wife Nancy, who apart from being master of the Apricot and the enemy of jargon has become a constructive commentator on my view of what marketing is about. As for most things in my life, I am deeply in her debt.

Professor Philip Kotler of Northwestern University has had a great influence on all marketing academics since the publication of his textbook *Marketing Management* in 1967, now in its fifth edition. All marketing educators are in his debt. I would like to thank Peter Spillard and my other colleagues in the Department of Marketing at Lancaster University for helpful suggestions and comments; Joyce Bisset for secretarial help; Joseph Staton, Librarian at the Institute of Practitioners of Advertising for never failing to respond to a request for information or data; and Hillary Gale and Sandra Hunsch for their research into cartoon material. Finally, Sue Corbett and Julia Mosse at Basil Blackwell and Penny Butler at the Economist Publications have been enthusiastic and understanding editors throughout.

Michael Thomas

Cartoons are reproduced by permission of *Punch*.

Foreword

Marketing is one of the most important, yet misunderstood, activities in modern life. Too many people think of marketing as the advertising and selling of goods, whereas in truth marketing starts long before the goods exist and continues long after the goods are sold. Marketers have the responsibility of helping their organizations figure out – through market research – what relevant groups of consumers and business buyers need, and then undertaking all of the activities – concept development and testing, product development, market testing, distribution planning, pricing, advertising and selling to make sure that the right goods reach the right buyers and create the right satisfaction. To accomplish all of this work efficiently, marketers must be familiar with economics, management science, psychology, sociology, and the mathematics of the marketplace.

It should therefore not be surprising that marketing has developed an elaborate and specialized vocabulary, as well as specialized usages of common market place terms. Michael Thomas has performed a great service in identifying the most important marketing terms that the intelligent layman will need to know. He not only defines each term but adds information about the use and ramifications of each term. His book also contains insightful quotes and cartoons to warm up the reader to the intriguing world of marketing.

In the past, marketers were primarily found in consumer packaged goods firms and in industrial firms. Now they are found in service industries (banks, airlines, hotels), nonprofit organizations (museums, hospitals, colleges, performing arts programmes), and the public sector (transportation, postal service, telecommunications). This points to an even stronger need for a well-constructed dictionary to facilitate understanding and discussion of marketing activities. Michael Thomas is to be congratulated for making this timely contribution.

Philip Kotler
Harold T. Martin Professor of Marketing
Northwestern University

Abbreviations

Here are some of the abbreviations commonly used in marketing. In many cases there are entries for them in the main text under the unabbreviated expression.

AA	Advertising Association (UK)
AAAA	American Association of Advertising Agencies
ABC	Audit Bureau of Circulation (USA, UK)
ACORN	A Classification of Residential Neighbourhoods (UK)
AMA	American Marketing Association (USA)
AMSO	Association of Market Survey Organizations (UK)
ARB	American Research Bureau
BARB	Broadcasters Audience Research Board (UK)
BBC	British Broadcasting Corporation
BRI	Brand Rating Index
CAM	Communication, Advertising and Marketing Education Foundation Ltd (UK)
CATI	Computer-assisted telephone interviewing
CIF	Cost, insurance, and freight
CO-OP	Co-operative Society
COMO	Committee of Marketing Organizations (UK)
CPM	Cost per thousand
CTNs	Confectioners, tobacconists and newsagents
DAGMAR	Defining advertising goals for measured advertising results
DIY	Do it yourself
DMU	Decision making unit
ECGD	Export Credits Guarantee Department
EFTPOS	Electronic fund transfer at point of sale
EPOS	Electronic point of sale
ESOMAR	European Society for Opinion and Marketing Research
FMCGs	Fast-moving consumer goods
FOB	Free on board
FTC	Federal Trade Commission (USA)
GATT	General Agreement on Tariffs and Trade
IBA	Independent Broadcasting Authority

ICS	Interviewer Card Scheme
IM	Institute of Marketing (UK)
IMRA	Industrial Marketing Research Association (UK)
IPA	Institute of Practitioners in Advertising (UK)
IPR	Institute of Public Relations (UK)
IPS	Institute of Purchasing and Supply (UK)
ISBA	Incorporated Society of British Advertisers Ltd (UK)
ISP	Institute of Sales Promotion (UK)
ITV	Independent Television (UK commercial TV)
JICNARS	Joint Industry Committee for National Readership Surveys (UK)
JICPAS	Joint Industry Committee for Poster Audience Surveys (UK)
JICRAR	Joint Industry Committee for Radio Audience Research (UK)
MCA	Market Research Corporation of America
MEAL	Media Expenditure Analysis Ltd
MFN	Most favoured nation
MINTEL	Market Intelligence Reports
MkIS	Marketing Information System
MORI	Market and Opinion Research International (UK)
MRS	Market Research Society (UK)
NAC	Nielsen Audience Composition
NCC	National Consumer Council (UK)
NPD	New product development
NTI	Nielsen Television Index
OCR	Optical character recognition
OCT	Over the counter
OFT	Office of Fair Trading (UK)
OTS	Opportunities to see
PIMS	Profit impact of market strategy
PR	Public relations
ROI	Return on investment
RPM	Resale price maintenance
RSGB	Research Surveys of Great Britain Ltd
SBU	Strategic business unit
SIC	Standard Industrial Classification
SWOT	Strengths, weaknesses, opportunities, threats
TGI	Target Group Index
TVR	Television rating

UNCTAD	United Nations Conference on Trade and Development
UPC	Universal product coding
USP	Unique selling proposition
VALS	Values and lifestyles (USA)
VAT	Value added tax (UK)

A

A Classification of Residential Neighbourhoods (ACORN). An identification of different types of neighbourhoods. ACORN was developed in the late 1970s by CACI Market Analysis Group, an Anglo-American market research firm, as a basis for SAMPLING and DIRECT MAIL. It works on the assumption that people living in particular types of neighbourhoods tend to exhibit similar patterns of behaviour. Marketers generally consider ACORN a better indicator of buyer behaviour than classifications based on occupation of head of household. It is used by companies seeking to identify where demand for their products may be concentrated, by major retailers for store location, and by bank and building societies for branch location. It is also in widespread use for selecting representative samples for questionnaire surveys.

There are 39 neighbourhood types in all, some of which, as examples, are as follows: agricultural villages; recent private housing, young families; modern private housing, older children; mixed owner-occupied and council estates; older private housing, skilled workers; unimproved terraces with old people; new council estates in inner cities; detached houses, exclusive suburbs.

Above the line. UK marketing jargon meaning mass MEDIA advertising expenditures. The term originated in the bookkeeping departments of ADVERTISING AGENCIES. Media expenditures which an agency makes for a client earn the agency a 15 per cent commission, whereas expenditures paid for by the client directly, such as special consulting or marketing research fees or money spent on SALES PROMOTIONS, are non-commissionable. The latter kind of expenditures gave rise to the term BELOW THE LINE which marketers use to mean sales promotion expenditures.

Account management group. The group within an ADVERTISING AGENCY responsible for the planning, supervision and coordination of all work done in the agency on a client's behalf. In modern agencies handling large accounts, this team will consist of an ACCOUNT MANAGER and an ACCOUNT PLANNER headed by an account director.

The work of the account management group starts with the ADVERTISING BRIEF worked out by the agency with the client detailing the objectives to be achieved. Strategy, or broad plans, are then drawn up showing how the objectives can be reached. From these broad plans, detailed ACTION PLANS are worked out and sent to the agency's various departments (see ADVERTISING AGENCY) for execution. The account management group coordinates the work of the departments and supervises the PRE-TESTING and modification of the rough copy until the final material is ready and the advertising campaign begins.

Account manager. The person in an ADVERTISING AGENCY responsible for a client's business. The account manager is the member of the ACCOUNT MANAGEMENT GROUP whose job it is to see that the objectives agreed upon by client and agency (see ADVERTISING BRIEF) are executed to everyone's satisfaction. He is the key figure in the agency's day-to-day relationship with the client and the person responsible for co-ordinating the work of all the agency's departments on the client's behalf, from beginning to end. The job is a challenging one, and the fall out rate high. If the client is not satisfied and the account is lost to the agency, the account manager has failed.

The term is also used in SALES MANAGEMENT. A sales representative acts as an account manager, arranging contacts between his own (the selling) organization and the buying organizations who are his customers and prospects. Account management has become a critical activity for many national brand manufacturers. See NATIONAL ACCOUNT MANAGEMENT.

Account planner. The member of an ADVERTISING AGENCY'S ACCOUNT MANAGEMENT GROUP whose job it is to see that all the work done by the agency for a client is based on an understanding of the people the work is intended to influence. MARKETING RESEARCH, therefore, is one of the main responsibilities of the account planner. From the account management team's first discussions of objectives and strategy, through the development of the creative ideas, to PRE-TESTING of ADVERTISING and campaign monitoring, the account planner will have up-to-date marketing research data at hand.

Account planning is a modern development which has elevated marketing research and integrated it with management, where, in agencies like Boase Massimi Pollitt and Abbot Mead

Vickers/SMS, it plays a very influential part in the agency's output (see below). Agencies differ, however, in the degree to which they practise account planning. In some it has a very limited role, or has simply meant renaming the old marketing research department.

The Account Group

Source: Boase Massimi Pollit.

Action plans. A term synonymous with the more familiar 'tactics'. Action plans describe exactly how strategies are to be implemented. They are the final rungs on PLANNING ladders, the schedules setting out what jobs are to be done, how, when, and by whom. An action plan for SALES PROMOTION support of a product over a year would typically show times and places for specific promotions (special sample offers, POINT OF SALE displays, COUPONS, etc.), trade shows to be attended, publicity releases, together with the amount of money budgeted for each element.

Adoption. The process by which consumers accept a new product, a new fashion, a new idea. The adoption process cannot begin until consumers are made aware of the new product (awareness stage); their interest in it must then be stimulated (interest stage), so that they consider the product in relation to their needs or desires (evaluation stage); then they try the product (trial stage) and finally continue to buy and use it regularly (adoption stage). (See DIFFUSION OF INNOVATION.)

> The codfish lays ten thousand eggs,
> The homely hen lays one
> The codfish never cackles
> To tell you what she's done –
> And so we scorn the codfish
> While the humble hen we prize.
> It only goes to show you
> That it pays to advertise.
>
> Anonymous

Advertising. Any communication which uses the MEDIA, is paid for by some interested party and is intended to inform and persuade. Information and persuasion are the objectives of all advertising, whether it be a 'lovely kittens for sale' notice in the classified section of the local paper or a company logo sewn on the sleeve of a champion tennis player or a two-minute commercial on television.

Advertising is an integral part of the MARKETING MIX, a vital element in the promotion of products and services to consumers. Though often maligned and misunderstood (it is *not* synonymous with marketing), advertising serves an important function in bringing customers and products together. It can establish beneficial relationships between products and customers and by reminding and reinforcing help to make those relationships last. Advertising is sometimes criticized for creating illusory needs and wants in people that companies can then satisfy to their profit. Whatever moral position one takes, it is certain that if a product is not perceived by the customer to provide some benefit, he will not continue to buy it, all the power of advertising notwithstanding.

Professional advertising is not haphazard. Different approaches or messages are required for different stages of the relationship between product and consumer. These stages are formalized as awareness, knowledge, liking, preference, conviction, and purchase (the HIERARCHY OF EFFECTS) and summed up by the mnemonic AIDA – Attention, Interest, Desire, Action. Over the course of a company's relationship with an ADVERTISING AGENCY, in some cases lasting for years, the advertising focus may be seen to move through these stages. Some of the best liked advertising is that intended to create awareness of a product, where the name of the brand is remembered because the advertisement has some very distinctive quality, very often humour. Examples are the television commercials for Cadbury's Smash, Heineken's lager, Listerine mouth wash, or Andrex toilet paper.

Advertising is not solely concerned with commercial products. Indeed, producers of goods and services account for only about half of the total amount spent on advertising. The remainder is spent by marketing intermediaries (retailers, banks), by all levels of government, by service organizations such as charities, and by individuals (classified advertising).

Advertising agency. Specialists in planning and handling ADVERTISING and SALES PROMOTION on behalf of clients. Although not all advertising agencies are alike, a large modern advertising agency will have an organization similar to that shown in the diagram below:

Organization of an advertising agency

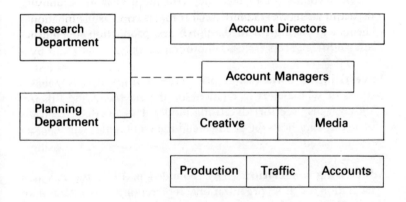

All the work an advertising agency does for a client (the 'account') is managed by an ACCOUNT MANAGEMENT GROUP, which consists of an account director (a senior manager who may supervise several accounts) and an ACCOUNT MANAGER. This team will draw on all the agency's departments to design and execute an advertising campaign.

The research department will provide marketing research

from SECONDARY DATA and research commissioned especially for each account's requirements. The planning department provides marketing advice for account managers. In ˙a few agencies ‚research and planning are integrated into the account management group in the person of the ACCOUNT PLANNER.

Many advertising ideas are born in the creative department. Often it is this department that gives an agency its distinctive competence.

The media department is responsible for planning advertising schedules and buying MEDIA space.

Television, cinema, and radio commercials and all material for print media are the job of the production department. Though some work may be subcontracted, all modern agencies have the capability of producing their own material.

The traffic department, sometimes called the control department, sees that each stage of the production process is completed on schedule, the deadlines being dictated by transmission or press dates.

The accounts (or finance) department, similar to accounting departments in most commercial firms, is responsible for billing clients and paying for media purchases, production subcontractors and freelancers (artists, photographers).

Advertising allowances. A price reduction given by manufacturers or wholesalers to retailers, on the understanding that the allowance is used for advertising locally. It is an effective means of advertising both the product and the retail outlet where it can be purchased.

Advertising association (AA). Founded in 1926, the AA is a federation of UK organizations representing the interests of advertisers, ADVERTISING AGENCIES and the MEDIA. It is the central spokesman for the UK advertising business, nationally and internationally.

The AA maintains a continuous programme of research and information retrieval. It collects and disseminates UK statistics on advertising expenditure and maintains a comprehensive library which is open to the public. It also runs an annual programme of seminars and training courses for people working in ADVERTISING, MARKETING, SALES PROMOTION and related fields.

Advertising brief. The statement of the objectives of an advertising campaign (also called the agency brief) agreed between an ADVERTISING AGENCY and a client, together with a brief history of the product (idea, organization, etc.) to be advertised. It is the starting point for the work of the agency's ACCOUNT MANAGEMENT GROUP.

The relationship between an agency and its clients is a delicate one. The client should determine the advertising objectives, plan overall advertising strategy and set the advertising budget, while the agency prepares and evaluates advertisements and develops the MEDIA plan. In practice, the chemistry of the relationship between client and agency determines the division of labour; strategy in particular may evolve by mutual agreement.

The advertising brief is critical because it represents the starting point in the agency–client relationship. Without a good brief, misunderstandings and confusion may result.

Advertising expenditure UK (£ million 1983–4). Tables 1 and 2 show the scale and scope of advertising in the UK. The illustration on pp. 8–9 shows the money spent on advertising by the ten biggest spenders in 1984 and their positions in 1983. Their products and the advertising agencies they use are also shown.

Table 1 *Total advertising expenditure by media (£ million)*

Media	1983	% of total	1984	% of total
National newspapers	584	16.3	678	16.7
Regional newspapers	817	22.8	921	22.7
Magazines & periodicals	224	6.3	250	6.2
Business & professional	276	7.7	311	7.7
directories	154	4.3	182	4.5
Press production costs	181	5.1	216	5.3
Total press	2236	62.5	2558	63.1
Television	1109	31.0	1245	30.7
Poster & transport	137	3.8	150	3.7
Cinema	16	0.4	16	0.4
Radio	81	2.3	86	2.1
Total	3579	100	4055	100

Source: Advertising Association, *Advertising Statistics Year Book 1985.*

1 Procter and Gamble

Expenditure £000s

1984 Total	1983	TV	%	Press	%	1983 Rank
48,948	52,932	48,782	99.7	166	0.3	1

Holding Company: Procter and Gamble Company USA.
Products: Ariel, Bold 3, Bounce, Daz, Fairy Liquid, Flash, Head and Shoulders, Lenor, Pampers, Vortex Bleach.
Agencies: Benton and Bowles, Greys, Leo Burnett, Saatchi and Saatchi.

2 British Telecom

Expenditure £000s

1984 Total	1983	TV	%	Press	%	1983 Rank
42,844	27,147	37,311	87.1	5,533	12.9	6

Formerly: British Telecommunications and British Telecommunications Yellow Pages.
Products: Business Phones, Call Stimulation, Corporate, Inphone, Yellow Pages.
Agencies: Abbott Mead Vickers, Ayer Barker, D'Arcy MacManus Masius, Davidson Pearce, Dorlands, Geers Gross, KMP.

3 Mars

Expenditure £000s

1984 Total	1983	TV	%	Press	%	1983 Rank
28,588	33,938	28,499	99.7	89	0.3	2

Holding Company: Mars Inc. USA.
Products: Mars Bars, Bounty, Marathon, Twix.
Agencies: Allen Brady and Marsh, D'Arcy MacManus Masius, Ted Bates.

4 Kelloggs

Expenditure £000s

1984 Total	1983	TV	%	Press	%	1983 Rank
26,992	28,471	25,479	94.4	1,512	5.6	3

Holding Company: Kellogg Company USA.
Products: All Bran, Branflakes, Corn Flakes, Crunchy Nut Cornflakes, Rice Krispies.
Agencies: J. Walter Thompson, Leo Burnett.

5 Pedigree Petfoods

Expenditure £000s

1984 Total	1983	TV	%	Press	%	1983 Rank
24,945	23,615	23,942	96	1,003	4	7

Holding Company: Mars Inc. USA.
Products: Chum, Chum Mixer, Kit E Kat, Pal, Whiskas Supermeat.
Agencies: D'Arcy MacManus Masius, Ted Bates.

6 Rowntree Mackintosh

Expenditure £000s

1984 Total	1983	TV	%	Press	%	1983 Rank
24,826	26,531	24,710	99.5	116	0.5	5

Products: Aero, Black Magic, Kit Kat, Rolo.
Agencies: J. Walter Thompson, Ogilvy and Mather, Saatchi and Saatchi.

7 Ford

Expenditure £000s

1984 Total	1983	TV	%	Press	%	1983 Rank
24,695	17,583	10,260	41.5	14,435	58.5	16

Holding Company: Ford Motor Company USA.
Formerly: Ford Cars and Light Vans Division and Ford Commercial Division.
Products: Escort, Fiesta, Orion, Sierra, Cargo Trucks, Transit Vans.
Agencies: Chetwynd Haddons, Lintas, Ogilvy and Mather.

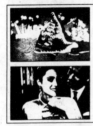

8 Nestle

Expenditure £000s

1984 Total	1983	TV	%	Press	%	1983 Rank
24,245	20,672	21,515	88.7	2,729	11.3	11

Holding Company: Nestle SA, Switzerland.
Products: Crosse and Blackwell Cook in the Pot, Crosse and Blackwell Dish of the Day, Libby's Um Bongo Juice, Nescafe Coffee, Nescafe Gold Blend, Nescafe Good Day Coffee, Milky Bar.
Agencies: Fairfields, Holmes Knight Ritchie, Leo Burnett, McCann-Erickson, Media Campaign Services.

9 Imperial Tobacco

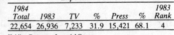

Expenditure £000s

1984 Total	1983	TV	%	Press	%	1983 Rank
22,654	26,936	7,233	31.9	15,421	68.1	4

Holding Company: Imperial Group.
Products: Grenville Cigars, Henri Wintermann Cigars, Lambert and Butler, Ogden Gold Block, Ogden St Bruno, Players Cigarettes and Cigars, Wills Cigarettes and Cigars.
Agencies: D'Arcy MacManus Masius, Geers Gross, Ogilvy and Mather, Sharps, Young and Rubicam.

10 Electricity Council

Expenditure £000s

1984 Total	1983	TV	%	Press	%	1983 Rank
20,733	21,720	14,922	72	5,811	28	9

Products: Central Heating, Cookelectric Cookers, Fridge Freezer, Tumble Dryer.
Agencies: Allen Brady and Marsh, Ayer Barker, Holmes Knight Ritchie, J. Walter Thompson, Ted Bates.

Source: Campaign, 7 June 1985.

Table 2   *Top 20 UK advertising agencies 1984*

Rank			Billings (£ million)		Staff	
1984	1983	Agency	1984	1983	1984	1983
1	1	Saatchi and Saatchi	162.00	134.00	600	570
2	2	J. Walter Thompson	142.00	131.50	573	558
3	4	Ogilvy and Mather	110.00	95.00	338	315
4	3	D'Arcy MacManus Masius	107.00	98.00	400	400
5	11	Dorland Advertising	102.00	60.40	365	275
6	7	Leo Burnett	82.40	72.30	242	241
7	9	Foote Cone and Belding	81.96	62.50	329	284
8	6	McCann-Erickson	78.70	72.60	314	312
9	10	Boase Massimi Pollitt	76.90	61.50	204	189
10	8	Young and Rubicam	76.72	66.50	308	316
11	14	Davidson Pearce	67.00	55.26	210	200
12	13	Benton and Bowles	66.10	54.75	213	231
13	5	Allen Brady and Marsh	64.15	76.76	277	349
14	15	Ted Bates	63.11	54.36	183	179
15	18	Doyle Dane Bernbach	61.00	49.00	230	228
16	12	Collett Dickenson Pearce	60.02	58.36	219	221
17	—	Crawford Halls Harrison Cowley	60.00	—	417	—
18	16	Lowe Howard-Spink	56.00	52.00	160	—
19	19	Grey Advertising	51.30	46.60	153	147
20	20	SSC and B Lintas	50.78	41.30	203	201

Source: Campaign, 11 January 1985.

Advertising expenditure USA ($ million 1983–4). The follow-ing tables show the scale and scope of advertising in the USA. Table 3 shows total advertising expenditure by media, Table 4 shows the 1984 expenditures of the 20 biggest spending US advertisers, and Table 5 shows the top 20 US advertising agencies.

Advertising Standards Authority (ASA). Legal, decent, honest and truthful – all advertisements in the UK are supposed to meet these criteria. As stated in the Code of Advertising Practice, advertisements must not mislead, misrepresent or offend. Anyone believing that an advertisement fails to meet these cri-teria is invited to complain to the ASA, the industry (-financed) watchdog committee. (Television advertising is under the con-

Table 3 *Total advertising expenditure by media (USA)*

Medium	1983 ($ million)	Per cent of total	1984 ($ million)	Per cent of total
Newspapers				
National	2,734	3.6	3,007	3.4
Local	17,848	23.5	20,737	23.5
Total	20,582	27.1	23,744	26.9
Magazines				
Weeklies	1,917	2.5	2,224	2.5
Women's	1,056	1.4	1.209	1.4
Monthlies	1,260	1.7	1,499	1.7
Total	4,233	5.6	4,932	5.6
Farm publications	163	0.2	181	0.2
Television				
Network	7,017	9.3	8,562	9.7
Spot	4,796	6.3	5,453	6.2
Syndicated barter	300	0.4	400	0.5
Cable (national)	320	0.4	400	0.5
Local	4,323	5.7	5.055	5.7
Cable (local)	30	0.0	40	0.0
Total	16,786	22.1	19,874	22.6
Radio				
Network	296	0.4	316	0.3
Spot	1,038	1.4	1.197	1.4
Local	3,876	5.1	4,300	4.9
Total	5,210	6.9	5,813	6.6
Direct mail	11,795	15.6	13,800	15.7
Business papers	1,990	2.6	2.270	2.6
Outdoor				
National	512	0.7	552	0.6
Local	282	0.4	310	0.4
Total	794	1.1	872	1.0
Miscellaneous				
National	7,331	9.6	8,546	9.7
Local	6,966	9.2	8,048	9.1
Total	14,297	18.8	16,594	18.8
Total				
National	42,525	56.1	49,590	56.3
Local	33,325	43.9	38,490	43.7
Grand total	75,850	100.0	88,080	100.0

Source: Advertising Age, 26 September 1985 (© Crain Communications Inc.).

Table 4   *Major US advertisers (1984)*

Rank	Company	Advertising ($)
1	Proctor & Gamble Co.	872,000
2	General Motors Corp.	763,800
3	Sears, Roebuck & Co.	746,937
4	Beatrice Cos.	680,000
5	R. J. Reynolds Industries	678,176
6	Philip Morris Inc.	570,435
7	American Telephone & Telegraph	563,200
8	Ford Motor Co.	559,400
9	K mart Corp.	554,400
10	McDonald's Corp.	480,000
11	J. C. Pennery Co.	460,000
12	General Foods Corp.	450,000
13	Warner-Lambert Co.	440,000
14	Ralston Purina Co.	428,600
15	PepsiCo Inc.	428,172
16	American Home Products	412,000
17	Unilever U.S.	395,700
18	International Business Machines	376,000
19	Anheuser-Busch Cos.	364,401
20	Coca-Cola Co.	343,300

Source: Advertising Age, 26 September 1985 (© Crain Communications Inc.).

trol of the INDEPENDENT BROADCASTING AUTHORITY.) Two-thirds of the Authority's Council must be unconnected with the advertising industry and its chairman must be independent.

Two recent examples illustrate how the Authority works. In one case a complaint was made against a company which had claimed in a local press advertisement that its Thirty Day Diet would have 'a devastating effect on unwanted fat'. The Authority upheld the complaint, the advertiser failing to produce evidence to support his claim. In another case a complaint was received about an advertisement in a farming journal for a portable hay cutter which featured a scantily clad female holding the device. The publishers said that they did not consider the advertisement offensive and had not themselves received any complaints. The ASA rejected the complaint, saying that although the approach could be found offensive by some, this particular advertisement had not caused widespread offence. These two

Table 5 *Top 20 US advertising agencies (1984)*

World income rank 1984	1983	Agency	World gross income ($ million) 1984	1983	US gross income ($ million) 1984	1983	World billings ($ million) 1984	1983	US billings ($ million) 1984	1983	US capitalised fees ($ million) 1984	1983	Total employees 1984	1983
1	1	Young & Rubican	480.1	414.0	323.1	274.4	3,202.1	2,761.4	2,155.1	1,830.1	0.0	0.0	8,418	7,745
2	2	Ted Bates Worldwide	424.4	387.9	263.2	244.4	2,839.2	2,586.1	1,754.7	1,629.0	237.7	185.2	5,345	5,124
3	4	Ogilvy & Mather International	421.0	345.8	270.5	204.1	2,887.9	2,360.4	1,804.3	1,361.4	0.0	0.0	7,428	8,030
4	3	J. Walter Thompson Co.	405.8	368.3	218.2	188.3	2,706.7	2,456.2	1,455.4	1,255.9	0.0	0.0	8,174	7,636
5	6	BBDO International	340.0	292.0	235.0	199.0	2,275.0	1,969.0	1,581.0	1,349.0	242.0	205.1	4,472	4,018
6	7	Saatchi & Saatchi Compton Worldwide	337.5	253.3	157.4	110.9	2,301.7	1,710.6	1,093.3	771.8	0.0	177.2	3,814	1,140
7	5	McCann-Erickson Worldwide	352.2	267.2	118.5	95.4	2,169.4	1,782.2	790.5	636.4	0.0	0.0	6,422	5,962
8	9	Foote, Cone & Belding Communications	268.5	208.4	196.9	158.9	1,802.2	1,405.6	1,324.4	1,075.5	0.0	0.0	5,832	4,468
9	8	Leo Burnett Co.	253.5	216.5	163.2	135.0	1,734.8	1,485.3	1,132.4	914.1	42.0	20.8	3,668	3,461
10	12	Grey Advertising	224.2	183.5	155.1	125.1	1,495.2	1,224.0	1,034.6	839.6	127.4	76.1	4,300	3,908
11	10	Doyle Dane Bernbach International	218.3	197.6	154.1	144.6	1,510.6	1,321.0	1,085.1	970.0	146.9	142.0	3,280	3,365
12	13	D'Arcy MacManus Masius Worldwide	198.6	173.0	106.9	91.6	1,337.6	1,156.5	712.9	61.03	0.0	0.0	3,583	3,626
13	11	SSC&B:Lintas Worldwide	182.9	155.5	62.6	50.8	1,230.3	1,047.5	414.6	338.7	0.0	0.0	3,765	3,705
14	14	Benton & Bowles	159.4	140.1	111.0	98.1	1,129.4	966.3	766.7	649.9	272.3	146.1	2,934	2,973
15	15	Marschalk Campbell-Ewald Worldwide	140.3	126.7	112.1	99.5	935.6	844.9	747.9	663.8	0.0	0.0	1,934	1,851
16	19	Needham Harper Worldwide	114.7	94.2	96.7	77.9	775.0	631.9	655.0	519.9	204.3	121.3	1,293	2,126
17	16	Dancer Fitzgerald Sample	110.4	105.0	109.2	94.1	758.0	726.1	750.2	627.0	0.0	0.0	3,352	3,175
18	18	N.W.Ayer	104.7	97.4	91.2	83.2	751.7	650.0	625.5	558.0	0.0	68.0	2,300	1,230
19	20	Wells, Rich, Greene	96.3	92.7	94.2	91.0	632.0	608.5	618.0	595.6	0.0	67.0	962	916
20	22	Bozell & Jacobs	94.2	74.4	92.5	73.5	671.0	557.0	660.0	551.0	114.0	86.0	1,650	1,350

Source: Advertising Age, 28 March 1985 (© Crain Communications Inc.).

HOW DARE THEY!

If you see an advertisement in the press, in print, on posters or a cinema commercial which makes you angry, write to us at the address below. (TV and radio commercials are dealt with by the I.B.A.)

The Advertising Standards Authority.
If an advertisement is wrong, we're here to put it right.

ASA Ltd, Brook House, Torrington Place, London WC1E 7HN.

examples illustrate the Authority's problem. In the first case, the misrepresentation is clear; in the second case, the question is one of interpretation – what can be deemed to constitute offence, to whom, and to how many before it offends under the code – and judgement consequently is far more difficult.

The advertising industry is well pleased with the way self regulation works, but consumer groups do not fully share this opinion. Unlike television commercials which must be shown to the Independent Broadcasting Authority before they can be aired, print advertising is not previewed by the ASA. The Authority, therefore, can only act after the fact, when consumers have complained (and in some cases been injured or inconvenienced).

In the USA, unfair or deceptive advertising – the FEDERAL TRADE COMMISSION stands in judgement – is subject to corrective advertising for which the advertiser must pay. (See NATIONAL ADVERTISING REVIEW BOARD.)

AIDA. Perhaps the oldest mnemonic in MARKETING, describing the stepping stones to successful communication: to get Attention, to hold Interest, to arouse Desire, and to obtain Action. (See HIERARCHY OF EFFECTS.)

American Association of Advertising Agencies (AAAA). Founded in the same year as the INSTITUTE OF PRACTITIONERS IN ADVERTISING (UK), 1917, and like it, the leading spokesman for the advertising agency business. It speaks on behalf of its agency members to the government, MEDIA owners and the general public and participates in industry self regulation through the NATIONAL ADVERTISING REVIEW BOARD.

Its members handle 75 per cent of all agency placed advertising in the USA.

It organizes meetings and seminars both regionally and nationally.

American Marketing Association (AMA). The premier organization of marketing managers and educators in the USA, founded in 1936. It has chapters all over the USA and sponsors a number of annual conferences. Its oldest journal, *Journal of Marketing*, has a circulation of over 25,000; *Journal of Marketing Research*, founded in 1904, and *Journal of Consumer Research*, founded in 1974, all have international reputations.

Association of Market Survey Organizations (AMSO). An association of 27 of the largest UK survey research organizations, accounting for nearly 80 per cent of UK research turnover. AMSO companies follow a Code of Standards, whose aim is to ensure the highest standards of market research work, and adhere to the industry's INTERVIEWER CARD SCHEME.

The Encyclopedia Galactica defines a robot as a mechanical apparatus designed to do the work of a man. The marketing division of the Sirius Cybernetics Corporation defines a robot as 'Your Plastic Pal Who's fun to be with'. The Hitch Hiker's Guide to the Galaxy defines the marketing division of the Sirius Cybernetics Corporation as "a bunch of mindless jerks who'll be first against the wall when the revolution comes . . ."

D. Adams, *The Hitch-hiker's Guide to the Galaxy*

Attitude. A point of view, made up of a set of beliefs and feelings, that influences a consumer's buying behaviour. A person who believes that it is right to 'Buy British' or 'Buy American' will present marketing problems to the Nissan Company. A person who values a healthy body will be a prospective consumer of wholefood products or buyer of sporting equipment.

The factors that make up attitude are complex. Marketers, however, especially advertising specialists, try to understand them so that PRODUCTS can be presented in a favourable light – or attitudes changed. When Honda decided to introduce their line of motorcycles into the American market they were faced with a generally hostile attitude toward the product: motorcycles were dangerous and associated with dangerous gangs. With advertising based on the slogan 'You meet the nicest people on a Honda', they were successful in changing people's attitudes and in selling their motorcycles.

Attributes. Features or characteristics associated with a PRODUCT which are important to consumers. For example, aroma, flavour, caffeine content and price might be considered the attributes of instant coffee; flavour, colour, smell, thickness, saltiness and texture might be attributes of chicken soup. Marketers try to describe their products in terms of attributes: instant coffees may be said to have 'an aroma of freshly percolated coffee' or 'the taste of ground coffee', while chicken soups may be 'thick and chunky' or 'taste like home-made' or 'have a low salt content'. Different consumers weigh the importance of a product's attributes differently – i.e. they look for different benefits. To one the saltiness of soup is the most important attribute while to another the texture counts most. The marketer's task is to communicate the particular attributes of his product as effectively as possible. (See CONJOINT ANALYSIS.)

Audience research. In the UK, research into television audiences is undertaken by the BROADCASTERS AUDIENCE RESEARCH BOARD and into commercial radio audiences by the JOINT INDUSTRY COMMITTEE FOR RADIO AUDIENCE RESEARCH. The BBC undertakes its own research through the BBC Audience Research Unit.

In the USA, national network television audience measurement is undertaken by A. C. NIELSEN Co., who prepare the Nielsen Television Index (NTI) and the Nielsen Audience Composition (NAC). Local television audience market research is done by American Research Bureau (ARB). ARB also provide data on radio audiences, as do Pulse Inc. Multi-media data is available from W. R. Simmons Associates and Brand Rating Index (BRI).

Audit Bureau of Circulation (ABC). Both the USA and the UK have an organization of this name. In the USA, the ABC is sponsored by national and local advertisers, advertising agencies and publishers. It publishes audited statements of newspaper and magazine circulation. FREESHEET circulation is monitored by Business Publications Audit of Circulation (BPA).

In the UK most newspapers and magazine publishers belong to the Audit Bureau of Circulation. The sales figures from publishers are audited and monthly circulation figures published quarterly in ABC's *Circulation Review*.

B

Banded pack. A SALES PROMOTION device similar to a quantity discount. Two or more items of the same product are bound together as a single pack and offered for sale at a price less than the combined price of the single items. Banded packs include the familiar 'Three for the price of two' or 'Buy two and get a third one free' offers.

Bar code. A product-coding device designed to be read by electronic scanners at the point of sale (see ELECTRONIC POINT OF SALE). The European bar code (see below) is composed of 13 digits. The first two digits identify the country issuing the code (the UK's number is 50). The next five digits are the manufacturer's number. The next five digits are the product item numbers, allocated by the manufacturer usually to the retailer. The last digit is the check digit, used by the computer to guard against misreading.

The retailer uses the five digits allocated to him by the manufacturer to price the product. Thus, when the bill is received at the electronic point of sale, it will show the customer what products have been purchased and how much they cost.

In the USA, bar codes are referred to as UNIVERSAL PRODUCT CODING, a misnomer since the system is not the one in universal use. Bar codes are being standardized worldwide by the Article Number Association.

Battle of the brands. In both the UK and the USA, a battle is going on between MANUFACTURER BRANDS and DEALER BRANDS.

Each is competing for shelf space in retail outlets, and as retailing, particularly grocery retailing, is concentrated in the hands of the very large chains that own the dealer brands, manufacturer brands seem to be at a clear disadvantage. Retailers not only control shelf space, naturally favouring their brands over competing manufacturer brands, but they can and do offer price advantages on their brands. In the manufacturers' favour is brand loyalty (supported by heavy advertising), pressuring retailers to carry their brands; retailers, however, have retaliated by packaging their brands to resemble very popular manufacturer brands. Dealer brand look-alikes stand on shelves beside such products as Johnson's Baby Powder and Nescafe.

The future for manufacturer brands is uncertain. If sales decline as a result of decreased exposure on retail shelves and price competition from dealer brands, the advertising budgets required to sustain brand loyalty will come under pressure.

Many manufacturers have responded by capitulating and becoming suppliers for dealer brands as well as their own. Others, like Kellogg, continue to resist. (See NATIONAL ACCOUNT MANAGEMENT.)

Below the line. A term used by UK marketers to mean SALES PROMOTION expenditures. (See ABOVE THE LINE.)

Benefit segmentation. The division of a market into groups of consumers who look for the same benefit from a PRODUCT. For example one segment of the toothpaste market consists of those who are chiefly concerned with preventing tooth decay (Crest's TARGET MARKET) and another of those whose primary concern is tooth brightness (Macleans' target market). (See MARKET SEGMENTATION.)

Blind test. A MARKETING RESEARCH technique in which two unidentified products are sampled by consumers who then indicate their preference. Blind testing is often used in new product research to test the product against an established brand. Because brand names and packages heavily influence consumers' PERCEPTION of products (see IMAGE), blind testing is the only way to measure such factors as taste, smell and texture on a comparative basis. For example, unlabelled California wines have been preferred in blind tests over unlabelled French wines by people who consider French wines superior.

Blind testing is a familiar feature of television commercials. Pepsi Cola ran a series of commercials called the Pepsi Challenge, in which it was claimed that a majority of people prefer Pepsi to Coke. These tests have helped Pepsi to raise its profile in markets where Coke means cola, but colas are not sold under blind-test conditions and on the shelf Pepsi has to compete with the brand name Coca Cola. In the USA Coke has about 45 per cent of the soft drinks market, Pepsi about 30 per cent.

Blind tests used in television advertising are required by law to be genuine.

Boston Box. See GROWTH/SHARE MATRIX.

Brand. A name, term, sign, symbol, mark, lettering or design (or any combination thereof) intended to differentiate a PRODUCT from its competitors. When marketed successfully, the brand name becomes a powerful force in the market place: Hoover, Tide, Mars, Kleenex, Campbell, Levi, for example, instantly identify products familiar to everyone. In markets where famous brands exist, competitors are always at a disadvantage. Only the strongest and/or cleverest survive (see POSITIONING and BRANDING.)

Brands may be used in different ways. Family brands are product names all containing the name of the company: Heinz Tomato Ketchup, Heinz Baked Beans (and so on 57 times), Cadbury's Fruit and Nut, Cadbury's Smash. Individual brands stand alone. Procter & Gamble's products all carry individual brand names: Tide, Bold, Cascade, etc. Some companies use different brand names for different PRODUCT LINES: Sears Roebuck, for example, sells appliances under the brand name Kenmore and tools under the brand name Craftsman. Brands may be owned by middlemen (see DEALER BRAND) or by manufacturers (see MANUFACTURER BRAND).

Brand loyalty. The much desired goal of all brand managers, namely sustained consumer commitment to a BRAND, the result of continuing satisfaction with the PRODUCT and effective and often heavy ADVERTISING. Strong brand loyalty reduces the impact of competitive brand promotions and discourages brand switching. (See HABIT and BRANDING.)

Brand management. Brand management, also known as product management, is in use by most leading consumer goods producers and some industrial goods producers. Developed in the 1930s by Procter & Gamble, it has developed into a widely accepted method for managing the marketing of individual brands in multi-product companies. (See diagram on p. 22.)

The brand manager usually has responsibility for a single brand: he or she becomes that product's champion and enthusiast in the company, setting the brand's marketing objectives, planning all the actions necessary to achieve those goals (TARGET MARKET identification, ADVERTISING, SALES PROMOTION, PACKAGING), scheduling and coordinating all the marketing activities and reporting to the product group management.

Most companies using the brand management system treat the brand manager as a PROFIT CENTRE.

Brand management is an ideal training ground for future marketing managers, and jobs as assistant brand managers are in great demand. (See MULTI-BRAND STRATEGY.)

Brand mapping. See PERCEPTUAL MAPPING.

Branding. Establishing in the minds of consumers a knowledge about and loyalty to a product focussed on the brand name. Branding produces advantages for a product. The brand name becomes associated with specific benefits, it enables the consumer to recognize the product on the store shelf, it helps to position the product relative to competing brands and it may help to insulate the product from price competition and to move it more easily through the DISTRIBUTION CHANNEL (see PUSH vs PULL STRATEGY). The primary tool for product branding is ADVERTISING.

Not all products are branded, however. For the advantages of unbranded products, see GENERICS.

British Rate and Data (BRAD). Published monthly, it provides information on circulation, cover price, RATE CARDS, copy and cancellation requirements for national and provincial newspapers,

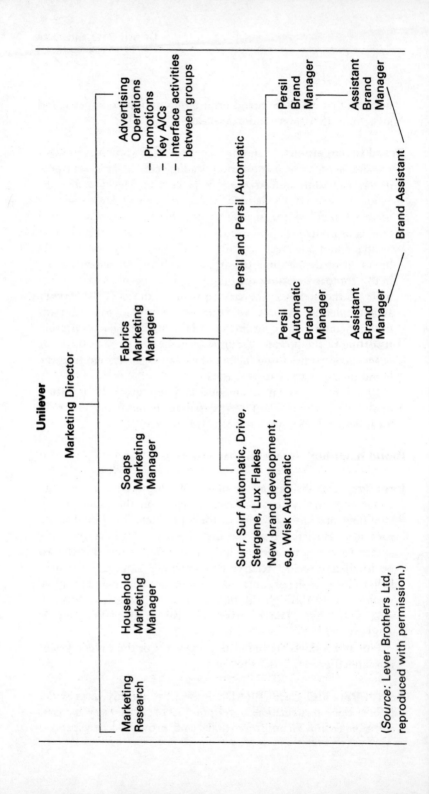

Unilever

Marketing Director

Marketing Research

Household Marketing Manager

Soaps Marketing Manager

Fabrics Marketing Manager

Advertising Operations
 – Promotions
 – Key A/Cs
 – Interface activities between groups

Surf, Surf Automatic, Drive, Stergene, Lux Flakes
New brand development, e.g. Wisk Automatic

Persil and Persil Automatic

Persil Automatic Brand Manager

Persil Brand Manager

Assistant Brand Manager

Assistant Brand Manager

Brand Assistant

(*Source*: Lever Brothers Ltd, reproduced with permission.)

for FREESHEETS, consumer, trade, technical and professional publications. Known as 'the Media Man's Bible'.

Broadcasters Audience Research Board (BARB). Provides weekly data on TV audiences (UK), based on over 3000 home panels covering all TV areas. Formerly known as the Joint Industry Committee for Television Audience Advertising Research (JICTAR).

Brokers. Marketing intermediaries who inform sellers of possible buyers and negotiate deals directly with buyers on a commission basis. They rarely have a continuous relationship with any one seller. They operate in the food, property, insurance, and stocks and bonds markets.

Bundling. Offering product-related services at a special rate to purchasers of a product. Banks that offer free checking/chequing or free safe deposit services to those who maintain high average balances in their accounts are bundling those services. Software is usually bundled with business computers. Bundling is a device to make the total PRODUCT more attractive to consumers.

Business gifts. One of the lubricants of good relations between business firms, varying in character and value from cases of wine to pens and pin-up calendars. (See FREE LUNCH.)

Business Monitor. A vital source of SECONDARY DATA on business activity, covering production, services and distribution, civil aviation and a miscellaneous category which includes such things as car registrations and cinema audiences. A GOVERNMENT PUBLICATION (UK).

Buygrid. A widely used MODEL of industrial buying situations (see Table 6), it identifies three classes:
  New task buying situations occur when the organization has no previous experience of the task.
  Modified rebuy describes a situation in which the organization reassesses its position, perhaps searching for quality improvements and cost reductions, usually triggered because of some dissatisfaction with existing supplies.

Straight rebuy requires little reassessment and usually entails reordering from the existing suppliers. (See ORGANIZATIONAL BUYING.)

Table 6 *The Buygrid analytic framework for industrial buying situations*

		Buyclasses		
		New task	Modified rebuy	Straight rebuy
B	1. Anticipation or recognition of a problem (need) and a general solution			
U				
Y	2. Determination of characteristics and quantity of needed item			
P	3. Description of characteristics and quantity of needed item			
H	4. Search for and qualification of potential sources			
A	5. Acquisition and analysis of proposals			
S	6. Evaluation of proposals and selection of supplier(s)			
E	7. Selection of an order routine			
S	8. Performance feedback and evaluation			

Source: P. J. Robinson, C. W. Faris and Y. Wind, *Industrial Buying and Creative Marketing* (Boston, Allyn & Bacon, 1947). Reproduced courtesy of P. J. Robinson.

Buying centre. In large industrial and commercial organizations, the group responsible for deciding what products to buy and what companies to buy them from. Typically it would consist of a purchasing agent, an engineer and a production manager. The buying centre will be involved in major purchasing decisions, involving such things as new machinery, computer systems, new raw material suppliers. (See ORGANIZATIONAL BUYING and BUYGRID.)

C

Cannibalization. A danger which exists when products or brands in a company's PRODUCT LINE are insufficiently differentiated or when competition among a company's brand managers becomes too intense (see BRAND MANAGEMENT). When increased sales of one brand result in decreased sales of another brand within the same product line, cannibalization has taken place.

Cannibalization is always a danger when a company extends a product line. Liquid Tide and Liquid Flash are being introduced as extensions to Tide and Flash, the original powdered products. If the extension brand reduces sales of the original brand but the combined sales are higher, the extension may be seen to have been successful. The danger remains, however, that the extension may weaken the brand name over time and result in a gradual loss of sales. Ideally, a new product should be sufficiently differentiated so that loss of sales does not occur in fellow brands.

Cash and carry wholesaling. A form of limited service wholesaling that has grown in recent years in both the USA and the UK. Cash and carry wholesalers perform the warehousing function traditional to wholesaling (they take delivery in bulk from manufacturers), but they keep no sales force, offer no delivery service, no credit, no merchandising nor reordering help, in short – no frills. Instead, the retailer goes to the warehouse, pays for his goods, and takes them away; the advantage to the wholesaler is lower costs, to the retailer lower prices.

The success of the 'cash and carry' in the grocery trade (predominantly in the UK) is a reflection of changes in consumer shopping patterns that heavily favour the large supermarket. The small independent retailers that offer customers convenience (the corner grocery, the village shop) have turned to the lower cost 'cash and carry' in order to keep their prices acceptable to their customers. Small restaurants, hotels and bed and breakfast establishments also depend heavily on the 'cash and carry'.

Cash cows. Strong brands which have high market shares in mature markets and which consequently produce a steady flow of cash for their companies. (See GROWTH/SHARE MATRIX.)

Catalogue stores. Stores which combine the techniques of catalogue selling with those of the discount house, dealing in national

BRAND products like jewellery, appliances, luggage, watches and hi-fi equipment. Customers who call at the store can view the merchandise, which may be displayed in locked glass cases, and order from catalogues. The inventory is stored behind the catalogue/showroom and customers' orders brought out to them. Customer comfort is not a first priority: lines/queues may form both for ordering and for collecting goods. Prices, however, are discounted and are therefore very competitive. The rapid growth of catalogue stores in recent years suggests that customers like them.

Argos is a well-known UK catalogue store as is Best Products Company in the USA.

Caveat emptor. Latin for 'let the buyer beware', a phrase which had legal significance in the days before modern consumer protection laws. In the absence of an express guarantee in a contract, the buyer purchased goods at his own risk. Today, consumers in the UK and the USA are protected by laws both in respect to manufacturers of products (see WARRANTY) and to retailers. Goods purchased from retailers must correspond with their description (be what they are said to be) and must be of merchantable quality and fit for their purpose (do what they are meant to do).

Chain stores. Chains are groups of retailers. A corporate chain consists of retail outlets owned and managed by one company, with central buying offices and centrally managed marketing, advertising and merchandising. F. W. Woolworth was one of the pioneers of the corporate chain store, opening his first store in America in 1879. Today the grocery business is increasingly dominated by chain stores – for example Sainsbury, Tesco and Asda in the UK, or Safeway, Kroger and A&P in the USA.

Chains may also be voluntary associations of retailers grouped around a wholesaler, such as IGA (USA) and Spar (UK) (see VOLUNTARY CHAINS).

The fastest growing retail chains in both Britain and America are associated with FRANCHISING operations such as McDonald's.

Channel captain. The most powerful member in the DISTRIBUTION CHANNEL (manufacturer to wholesaler to retailer). Traditionally, the channel captain has been the manufacturer, such as Austin Rover (UK) or General Motors (USA), dominating their dealer networks, but there have always been retailers who have been channel captains. F. W. Woolworth, for example, in its heyday controlled the full length of the channel of distribution: manufacturers made goods to Woolworth's specifications. Marks and Spencer today is a classic example. Wholesalers, too, can be channel captains, for example Spar in the UK and IGA in the USA, both working with independent retailers (see VOLUNTARY CHAINS). In many distribution chains there is no obvious channel captain; indeed, members of the chain or channel, particularly retailers, may not even recognize that they are part of a distribution system.

Channel conflict. Disagreement between members of a DISTRIBUTION CHANNEL. It may be horizontal or vertical conflict. Horizontal channel conflict can occur among retailers, where one retailer feels that another is competing too vigorously or is invading his territory with ADVERTISING. Vertical channel conflict occurs between retailers and their suppliers (manufacturers) when either side feels itself unduly dominated by the other.

Cognitive dissonance. In marketing terms, the dissatisfaction which arises when there is a difference between a consumer's expectations of a PRODUCT and the product's performance. Since consumers' expectations about products are largely built by ADVERTISING, this dissonance may be reduced by making claims consistent with product performance. Offers of guarantees, WARRANTIES, and after-sales service can reassure a consumer that any source of dissatisfaction will be put to rights.

Cold calling. Calling on a customer without a prior appointment. Many retail businesses expect sales representatives to drop in regularly; in that context it is a custom which works satisfactorily. For most kinds of selling, however, it is unwelcome, inefficient and time wasting. Where it is unavoidable, such as in house-to-house selling, the hit rate (the number of calls that are made before a customer makes a purchase) is very low.

Committee of Marketing Organizations (COMO). A UK body formed to encourage the development of MARKETING as a discipline in all sectors of business, COMO represents the main organizations in the UK that are concerned with marketing: i.e. ADVERTISING ASSOCIATION (AA), ASSOCIATION OF MARKET SURVEY ORGANIZATIONS (AMSO), COMMUNICATION, ADVERTISING & MARKETING EDUCATION FOUNDATION LTD (CAM), Incorporated Advertising Management Association (IAMA), INCORPORATED SOCIETY OF BRITISH ADVERTISERS (ISBA), INDUSTRIAL MARKETING RESEARCH ASSOCIATION (IMRA), INSTITUTE OF EXPORT (IE), INSTITUTE OF MARKETING (IM), INSTITUTE OF PACKAGING (IP), INSTITUTE OF PRACTITIONERS IN ADVERTISING (IPA), INSTITUTE OF PUBLIC RELATIONS (IPR), INSTITUTE OF PURCHASING AND SUPPLY (IPS), INSTITUTE OF SALES PROMOTION (ISP), MARKET RESEARCH SOCIETY (MRS), MARKETING SOCIETY (MS), Public Relations Consultants Association (PRCA).

Communication, Advertising and Marketing Education Foundation Ltd (CAM). Formed in 1969, CAM is an educational charity providing education and training in communications, public relations, advertising and marketing. It is supported principally by the ADVERTISING ASSOCIATION and the INSTITUTE OF PUBLIC RELATIONS.

Communications strategy. Marketers may communicate directly with the market place by means of face-to-face communication between a sales person and a potential customer or they may rely more on indirect or non-personal communication, using ADVERTISING and SALES PROMOTION. The nature of the PRODUCT and its market influences a company's communications strategy. If the company's products are targeted at mass consumer markets and the company can afford it, heavy MEDIA advertising is the strategy called for – communication directly with the consumer to create consumer demand. Small and/or poorer companies without the resources to advertise may have to use PERSONAL SELLING at each stage in the DISTRIBUTION CHANNEL in order to get their products to the consumer (see PUSH *vs* PULL STRATEGY).

Industrial marketing generally calls for personal selling to meet the often highly specialized needs of industrial customers.

Whatever the circumstances of the firm, it is important that it should develop an effective communications strategy.

Comparative advantage. An explanation, first formulated by the British economist David Ricardo (1772–1823), of why trade takes place between nations. He argued that each nation has a different endowment of the factors of production, which he defined as being land and labour, and that each nation should specialize in the production of those goods requiring the use of its most abundant factor. Thus England, he argued, should specialize in wool production since its land and climate were good for sheep, while Portugal should specialize in wine, requiring a warm climate and more intensive use of labour.

This theory, much developed by economists, still holds currency, though it appears to have little explanatory value in today's world where most trade appears to take place between nations that have relatively similar factor endowments. The factors of production are now identified as land, skilled and unskilled labour, capital, technology and entrepreneurial skill.

Competitive advantage. A factor which places a firm at an advantage over its rivals. ME-TOO products in a crowded product field command no significant consumer preference. Competitive advantage may be secured in a number of ways: by INNOVATION in product and product design, by distinctiveness in ADVERTISING, promotion or selling, by superior methods of distribution, by superior quality, or by lower price as a result of more effective management of the MARKETING MIX. Cutting price as a means of gaining competitive advantage, though tempting, is a short-term tactic which is usually unwise: competitors can quickly respond with price cuts of their own. Competitive advantage should not be ephemeral nor easily copied by rivals.

Computer–assisted telephone interviewing (CATI). Telephone interviewing which is conducted by an interviewer using a computer and a computerized QUESTIONNAIRE. The interviewer reads the questions from the computer's visual display unit and keys in the respondent's answers. Since the computer can follow complex questionnaire routing very efficiently (if the answer to question 10 is NO, then go to question 15), interviewer error is reduced. Data processing is also very much faster.

Concentrated segmentation. Some companies, particularly

smaller companies, identify a comparatively small segment of the market on which to concentrate their marketing effort. By selecting a niche in the market for themselves, they hope to avoid head on competition with larger and more powerful rivals. A classic example of a successful product in a small market is the hand-made Morgan sports car (UK), the demand for which keeps the company's order books filled. Rolls Royce, though a much larger company, has been equally successful in catering to a small but affluent segment of the international market. A California company has found a niche providing personalized coach transportation for pop stars who spend much of their lives 'on the road'.

Niche marketing, as concentrated segmentation is sometimes called, is currently very popular. It is no guarantee of a safe haven, however, since mass marketers will only ignore niches as long as they see no way to compete in them profitably and as long as they are not threatened by them. Should an opportunity or a threat be detected, however, the market power of the mass marketer would prove very uncomfortable for the nicher.

Concept testing. A technique used to test new ideas and concepts at an early stage in NEW PRODUCT DEVELOPMENT. QUALITATIVE RESEARCH techniques, such as GROUP DISCUSSION, can yield valuable insights into how consumers might perceive a new product idea, what it would be like, how it might be used, when and by whom. For example, a group of housekeepers might be brought together and asked to explore the concept of robotic housekeeping.

Conjoint analysis. A technique used in NEW PRODUCT DEVELOPMENT. A company might see an opportunity to introduce a new product into the market (see PERCEPTUAL MAPPING), but will have to decide what particular features and qualities to give that product so that it can be properly positioned in respect to its competitors (see POSITIONING). Every product has a large number of ATTRIBUTES, some of which are more important than others, and some combinations of which are more important than others. Conjoint analysis is a technique for testing the strength of various combinations of features to develop a picture, not of an ideal product necessarily, but of the combination of attributes that are strongest (best liked) in the perception of consumers. For example, a motor-car company planning a new model might want to know what features of car design are most important to prospective buyers. Various features might be tested, such as electronic performance monitoring, style, seating comfort, riding comfort, boot/trunk space, back seat space, safety.

The technique may also be used when product modifications are being considered and when REPOSITIONING is thought desirable.

Conjoint analysis is a development of a simpler technique called TRADE-OFF ANALYSIS. (See PAIRED COMPARISONS.)

Consumer market. The market for CONSUMER PRODUCTS. It is distinguished from the industrial market where buyers of goods are not the end users.

Consumer panel. See DIARY PANEL.

Consumer products. Products purchased for consumption by the ultimate user. Industrial products are purchased in order to facilitate the production of some other good. When a student buys a paper clip, it is a consumer product; when a university supplies department buys a gross of paper clips, they are industrial products, used to facilitate the provision of education.

Consumer profile. A description of the age, social class and other characteristics of consumers of a given product or BRAND (see Table 7). Consumer profiling is an essential exercise in developing COMMUNICATIONS STRATEGY and MARKET SEGMENTATION.

Table 7 *A profile of the consumers of Hirondelle wines (1976)*

Sex (%)		Social class (%)					Age (%)					
Men	Women	AB	C1	C2	D	E	15-24	25-34	35-44	45-54	55-64	65+
50.6	49.4	41.2	32.0	18.5	6.2	2.0	24.1	28.4	17.9	13.8	10.5	5.2

Source: Kenneth Simmonds, *Strategy and Marketing* (Philip Allan Publishers, 1982), p. 140.

Consumer protection. In the UK, consumer protection is well institutionalized. The OFFICE OF FAIR TRADING carries the primary responsibility for safeguarding consumer rights, and the NATIO-NAL CONSUMER COUNCIL represents consumers' interests to government. Individual consumer problems are handled by a variety of organizations such as Citizens' Advice Bureaus, Consumer Advice Centres, the Trading Standards Departments of local authorities and the Consumer Councils of the nationalized industries.

There are several Federal agencies in the USA which have an impact on the marketing activities of companies. The most notable are the FEDERAL TRADE COMMISSION, the Food and Drug Administration, the Consumer Products Safety Commission, the Environmental Protection Agency and the Office of Consumer Affairs.

Consumer Reports. The magazine of the American Consumers Union, an independent product testing agency. The British equivalent is *WHICH?*, the organ of the Consumers' Association.

Consumerism. President John F. Kennedy issued a 'Consumer Bill of Rights' in 1962. It never became law, but its identification of the right to safety, the right to be informed, the right to choose and the right to be heard inspired a consumer movement in the 1960s that has had an impact on the market place in both the USA and the UK. Consumerism attempts to counterbalance the power of manufacturers, advertisers and retailers by ensuring that consumer rights are clearly defined and insisting that they be adequately protected.

Ralph Nader gained fame as a champion of consumer rights in the 1960s in the USA, beginning with his pursuit of General Motors and their 'unsafe at any speed' Corvair. Nader's campaign led to the enactment of the Traffic and Motor Vehicle Safety Act (1966). In the UK, consumerism has few obvious battle honours, although the establishment of the OFFICE OF FAIR TRADING (1973) was probably a partial response to the consumerist lobby. (See CONSUMER PROTECTION.)

Convenience stores. Retail outlets, commonly called 'C-stores', that trade primarily on the appeal of convenience offered to customers. They offer products based upon a knowledge of local consumer needs, are open long hours, and are located conveniently near their customers. Convenience is clearly one way for the small business to counter the growth of the grocery chains. It is predicted that there will be over 5000 new C-stores in the UK by the end of 1987.

C-stores are not confined to single-unit, independent outlets. A very successful American chain, 7–Eleven, has 7500 branches in the USA and expects to have between 80 and 90 outlets in the UK by the end of 1986. In addition to carrying a range of convenience products, they offer fast food and snacks.

Co-operative Movement. The Co-operative Movement in the UK dates from 1844 when the Rochdale Society of Equitable Pioneers was founded as a retail grocery (food) store by a group of consumers, based on open membership and democratic control. Members shared the profits from the retailing business in the form of dividends calculated from the amount of money each member had spent in the Society's store. The Rochdale co-operative model spread throughout Europe.

In the UK the Co-operative Wholesaling Society, serving an extensive network of retail 'Co-op' shops, is still a significant factor in retailing (see GROCERY MARKET SHARES and RETAILERS). Some consumer and agricultural co-operatives were established in the USA in the nineteenth century, but the movement did not succeed. In recent years there have been some attempts to re-establish small-scale co-operative retailing.

Corporate image. What the public thinks about a company. Companies typically like to project themselves as good employers, caring about people, reliable, or uncompromising in the pursuit of excellence. DuPont's image as a company in the forefront of progress has been nurtured by more than 50 years of advertising based on the slogan, 'Better living through chemistry'. In recent years, corporate advertising has grown, often attempting to present a company in a light compatible with the social morality of the day. Oil companies, for example, are at pains to be seen as environmentally responsible, and public utilities emphasize their commitment to public service (see INSTITUTIONAL ADVERTISING).

A good corporate image not only helps to sell a company's products, but it is also an advantage to a company in its relations with government, unions, other companies, and the public.

Corporate logo. Company emblems or signs, many of which become as familiar and powerful as BRAND names. The Bell Telephone, former logo of AT&T (American Telephone and Telegraph Corporation) and famous throughout the USA, was a dramatic casualty of the recent splitting up of the corporation. The courts decided that none of the resulting new companies had the right to use the logo, and it was withdrawn from use.

Corporate plan. The broad objectives and strategies to be pursued by a company over a period of time, often five years. The corporate plan might support new product development as a means of obtaining growth in the future, or it might explore the rationale for new market development, product acquisition and diversification.

A typical corporate plan is one recently announced by Rank Xerox (UK). It aims to diversify from its copier base and identifies system compatibility and document management as areas for future growth. New products are to be added by acquisition – microcomputers and word processors – and new products and services are to be developed, such as networking and communications products and data management services for business and government. The sales force is to be retrained for SYSTEMS SELLING, and revenues from systems products are to be increased from 20 per cent to 50 per cent in the 1990s. (See PLANNING.)

Cost per thousand (CPM). A convenient way to compare the costs of different MEDIA, by calculating how much it would cost, using each medium, to reach 1000 people. For example, for magazines and newspapers, the CPM (sometimes CPT in the UK) is calculated as

$$\frac{Cost \times 1000}{Circulation}$$

If the cost of a full page advertisement in a magazine is £2000 and the magazine's circulation is about one million copies, the cost of

Some corporate logos

ALLIED┬LYONS	Distillers	NABISCO BRANDS
American Motors	DU PONT	National Panasonic
AVIS	Eastman Kodak	Nestlé
BRITISH AIRWAYS The world's favourite airline.	Gallaher	PROCTER & GAMBLE
BP British Petroleum	Gillette	Rowntree Mackintosh
Gervais Danone	IBM	Smith+Nephew
Cadbury Schweppes	International Playtex, Inc.	UB UNITED BISCUITS
Chesebrough-Pond's	Johnson&Johnson	Wrangler

Source: Saatchi and Saatchi Co. PLC *Annual Report*, 1984.

reaching 1000 people is about £2. The general formula for television is

$$\frac{Cost \times 1000}{TV \text{ ratings}}$$

RATE CARDS set out the advertising rates for each medium.

CPM, however, is only a first approximation of cost. What matters most to the marketer is not the cost per thousand people reached but the cost per thousand prospective customers effectively reached. (See MEDIA PLANNING.)

Cost-plus pricing. A simplistic approach to price-making still used by many companies. In cost-plus pricing the manufacturer sets his selling price by taking fixed costs plus variable costs and adding some 'acceptable' margin of profit (mark up). The wholesaler marks up the manufacturer's price and sells to the retailer who in turn marks up the price to the customer by another profit margin addition. The predictable outcome of the procedure is a retail selling price which bears little relation to consumer demand for the product. In contrast, the market-oriented producer finds the price that is acceptable to the market place, deducts retail and wholesale mark up, and then examines the possibility of producing the product at a profit, given the costs of production.

Counter trading. In international trading, particularly that between the Eastern and Western Bloc countries, where the former are usually short of hard currency (sterling or dollars), counter trading has developed as a means by which the Eastern Bloc countries can pay for the goods they buy from the West. It may take the form of barter, as when the Soviet Union paid for Pepsi Cola with vodka; compensation deals (payment partly in goods, partly in an acceptable currency); counter purchase (payment in money but only on the understanding that the money is used to purchase the buying country's goods); and buy back deals, as when a country exporting a chemical plant or machinery for making television tubes accepts partial payment in the form of output from the factory.

Coupons. Certificates which give consumers price reductions on specific products. They can be included in print advertising, mailed to the householder or enclosed in or printed on a product's package. In the USA coupons are heavily utilized by consumer goods' manufacturers, despite the fact that their redemption rate is less than five per cent; city newspapers may have large shopping sections with coupon offers in their Thursday and Friday editions, and Sunday newspapers frequently include coupon inserts.

Coupons are commonly used to encourage the purchase of a new product. When they are used to stimulate sales of a mature product, they represent a form of price reduction that is more subtle than straightforward price cutting – and less likely to be noticed by competitors!

Malredemption can be a problem for manufacturers who use coupons. Retailers may redeem the coupons from the manufacturer but give the price reduction on products other than the couponed ones. (See SALES PROMOTION.)

Customer service. An element in a company's product policy (see MARKETING MIX), since very few products are sold today that have no customer-service element. Customer service is designed to enhance the appeal of a product, often becoming a way of differentiating a product from its competitors. In general, the more technologically complicated a product is, the more important the service component becomes. In the sales of industrial goods and consumer products such as computers and cars, the service component may be at least as important as the product itself to prospective customers.

Customer-service offerings take a variety of forms: after-sales service, such as repair and replacement service and/or guarantees; credit; technical advice; ease of contact (toll-free phone numbers in the USA); complaints and adjustments policies; maintenance service and contracts; and information services. Where products are leased to customers, service is an integral part of the LEASING agreement.

All customer service has as its objective the establishment of a lasting relationship between buyer and seller.

D

Dagmar. An acronym standing for Defining Advertising Goals for Measured Advertising Results. DAGMAR was developed in a report written by Russell Colley in 1961 for the Association of National Advertisers (USA), which has been the subject of argument among marketers. Colley argued that it was the job of ADVERTISING to communicate and that its success or failure should be measured against the specific objectives defined for it. Critics, however, point out that advertising is not an end in itself but only a component of the MARKETING MIX where sales figures are the only significant measure of success.

Date stamping. A legal requirement in both the UK and the USA that perishable food products should show on their packaging the date by which the product should be sold to the consumer.

Dealer brand. A product on which a middleman, usually a retailer, puts his own BRAND name, such as Sainsbury and St Michael (Marks and Spencer) in the UK, and Kenmore and Craftsman (Sears Roebuck) and Ann Page (A&P) in the USA.

The increasing success of dealer brands reflects the growing power of retail chains. Major manufacturers with their own established national brands are now forced to negotiate the supply of their own products to the major chains to be sold under dealer brand names (see BATTLE OF THE BRANDS).

Other terms for dealer brand are 'private label' and 'own label' (UK) and 'distributor brand' (USA).

Decision-making unit (DMU). See BUYING CENTRE.

Demarketing. The process of discouraging consumers from buying or consuming. Governments demarket cigarettes by requiring that health warnings be printed on every pack. 'Share your bath with someone tonight' was a creative and well-received slogan used by the Water Authority (UK) to demarket water during a recent summer drought. Raising price or restricting distribution as a form of rationing can be regarded as demarketing.

Demographics. Facts about the composition of the population (age, sex, family size, FAMILY LIFE CYCLE, income, occupation,

education, religion, race and nationality). Demographic analysis reveals important information affecting consumer demand, such as changes in class structure, family composition, and age group balance. The baby boom of the 1960s provided marketing opportunities for food manufacturers such as Heinz and Gerber ('Babies are our only business') and Johnson & Johnson (baby powder and shampoo). As the birth rate fell off and the numbers of elderly people increased, new opportunities were perceived: Gerber switched to insurance ('Gerber now babies the over-50s') and Johnson & Johnson REPOSITIONed their baby powder and shampoo as adult products. The increase in the numbers of working mothers and the growth of the Hispanic population in the USA and the Asian and West Indian populations in the UK are other demographic factors with important marketing implications.

Demographic data provide a basis for MARKET SEGMENTATION. Products may be targeted for different age groups (toys for children, cosmetics for teenagers or for the middle aged), different sexes (Marlboro cigarettes for men, Virginia Slims for women, different magazines for men and women), different income groups (designer clothes and high-street clothes), etc.

Department stores. Stores traditionally located in the heart of central shopping areas in large cities, carrying a wide range of PRODUCT CLASSES, typically clothing, home furnishings and household goods, and giving much attention to display and service. To support high rental locations and heavy staffing, department stores have operated on a high mark-up basis. In recent years many department stores have closed, reflecting heavy price competition from both discounters and self-service stores selling similar product categories. They have also been affected by the decline of central city shopping areas, with the result that many have opened up satellite stores in suburban shopping centres (see WHEEL OF RETAILING and PLANNED SHOPPING CENTRES).

The first department store is thought to have been the Bon Marché, opened in Paris in 1852.

Depth interview. An unstructured personal MARKETING RESEARCH interview in which respondents talk freely under prompting and guidance from a researcher, usually a psychologist, who tries to uncover deep or hidden levels of motivation and behaviour. Projective techniques developed by clinical psychologists, such as word association and sentence or story completion, may be used. The depth interview requires highly skilled interviewers and is very costly, but it is the major tool of MOTIVATION RESEARCH.

Derived demand. A valuable concept in marketing, drawn from economics. Industrial marketers do not sell directly to consumers but to intermediary manufacturers. The demand for industrial goods and services is thus derived from the demand for the consumer goods which require the intermediary product; for example, the demand for the machinery to make cans is derived from the demand for the products packaged in cans.

Desk research. MARKETING RESEARCH using SECONDARY DATA, usually the first stage in any marketing research project. Researchers try to learn as much as possible about a subject using information already available before beginning field work for the collection of PRIMARY DATA. (See OFF-THE-PEG RESEARCH.)

Diary panel. Panel research is an important part of the business of major marketing research agencies in the UK. Diary panelists are shoppers who use diaries to keep a regular (daily, weekly, etc.) record of all purchases of all or selected products. Attwoods consumer panel, in existence in the UK since 1948, consists of 4800 households and covers all household purchases. The Market Research Corporation of America (MCA) uses 7500 families located throughout the USA who note all food and drug purchases on a weekly basis. The analysis of data in these diaries is offered for sale.

Differentiated marketing. Providing products to meet the specific needs of different consumer segments (see MARKET SEGMENTATION). As a consequence of differentiated marketing, weight-watching cola drinkers can buy diet colas, bedtime coffee drinkers can buy decaffeinated coffee, and students can fly stand-by. Good marketing brings about as perfect a match as possible between a segment of the market and the product to serve that market.

Diffusion of innovation. The process by which new products and services reach customers. Initially, only individuals who are wholly confident about the new product, or who like taking risks, will buy. Once the INNOVATORS have adopted the new product, a larger group, the early adopters, will come into the market. These early adopters will be OPINION LEADERS who will influence wider consumer acceptance of the product.

MARKETING RESEARCH techniques can track how a product is spreading, who has started and who is continuing to use it. The supplier can use this information to direct promotional effort to the right group of customers. Great successes include central heating, double glazing and home computers.

Diffusion can be speeded up by making adoption seem less risky. Cosmetics manufacturers give samples away free or at an introductory price. A manufacturer may install a machine on a six-month trial basis with a buy-back guarantee or, in IBM's case, give away thousands of PCs to US business schools in order to secure consumer acceptance and develop BRAND LOYALTY. (See ADOPTION.)

Direct mail. The sending of advertising and promotional material directly to consumers. Usually associated with MAIL ORDER selling, it nevertheless covers a wide field, including appeals for money and political communications.

The great advantage of direct mail is that the marketer can target his audience with great precision. In the USA, for example, Life Style Selector, a Denver based company, has a data base of ten million names and addresses, each identified by DEMOGRAPHIC and consumption information, making it possible for marketers to select the most likely buyers of virtually any product.

Direct mail is used by such well-known organizations as the *Reader's Digest*, the Franklin Mint, Time-Life, *The Economist* (UK), the Automobile Association (UK), the Consumers' Association (UK) and Thomas Cook.

Though direct mail is sometimes disparagingly referred to as 'junk mail', recent research suggests that less than one mailing in five goes into the waste bin. It is the UKs third largest mass medium, with a 22 per cent growth rate in 1984.

Direct marketing. The shortest channel of distribution – when a manufacturer or producer deals directly with the consumer. The farmer who advertises 'Potatoes for sale' at his gate, or 'Pick your own fruit', is engaging in direct marketing, as is the sales representative who calls at your home (Avon Cosmetics, *Encyclopedia Britannica*). MAIL ORDER is the largest category of direct marketing, very successfully used by Littlewoods (UK) and Sears Roebuck (USA). Two other forms of direct marketing are TELEPHONE SELLING, widespread in the USA, and direct selling to the consumer through the MEDIA.

Directional policy matrix. The PRODUCT portfolio matrix developed by Shell International (see Table 8). It is based on two dimensions: the profitability of the market segment in which the business operates and the competitive position of the business in this segment. The factors that determine these two dimensions are flexible and therefore can be made relevant to a particular industry. The strategy recommendations are not unlike those generated by the GROWTH/SHARE MATRIX. (See PORTFOLIO ANALYSIS.)

Table 8 *The Shell International Directional Policy Matrix*

Company's competitive capabilites	Prospects for sector profitability		
	Unattractive	Average	Attractive
Weak	Disinvest	Phased withdrawal Custodial	Double or quilt
Average	Phased withdrawal	Custodial Growth	Try harder
Strong	Cash generation	Growth Leader	Leader

Source: Shell Chemical Co., reproduced with permission.

Discount stores. Stores which sell MANUFACTURER BRANDS at low prices. They are able to keep prices lower than more traditional retail outlets because they keep their costs lower: they are generally located in low rent areas, their layout and decor is very functional, they are largely self service and they buy in large quantities directly from manufacturers, thereby obtaining QUANTITY DISCOUNTS. Fast stock turnover (see STOCK CONTROL) is the key to their success.

Distribution. A key marketing function – the process of getting products to consumers. Although some manufacturers can and do sell direct to consumers (see DIRECT MARKETING), practical considerations require most to use a distribution system composed of independent MIDDLEMEN, usually wholesalers and retailers. These intermediaries carry out critically important marketing activities, such as buying and selling, sorting and storing, transporting and financing products as they move from producer to consumer – all necessary functions if products are to be found by consumers in the right place, at the right time, at the right price.

Distribution centre. Manufacturer-owned warehousing, receiving goods in bulk and despatching them to retail outlets. Of growing importance in the DISTRIBUTION CHANNEL, a modern distribution centre is computer controlled and often robotically equipped in order to speed up inventory turnover. Distribution centres draw goods from several production centres and are particularly important in international trade.

Distribution channel. The network of firms performing the functions necessary to move goods or services from manufacturer to consumer, primarily wholesalers and retailers. (See DISTRIBUTION, CHANNEL CAPTAIN and CHANNEL CONFLICT.)

Distributor. Wholesaler of industrial products. Distributors are the major force in industrial distribution channels, and even in the USA most have continued to survive as relatively small units of business. They sell manufactured goods to manufacturers, providing warehousing and a range of services such as delivery, credit, order processing and technical advice. In their capacity as sellers to manufacturers, they must be able to respond quickly to their customers' needs so that production will not be disrupted. As part of their quick-response capability, many distributors provide a repair service for the goods they sell, acting on behalf of manufacturers.

Distributor brand. See DEALER BRAND.

Do-It-Yourself (DIY). Known as DIY in the UK, do-it-yourself home decoration and house maintenance has become a very popular way to save money. The retail sector has responded with stores using supermarket techniques to provide DIY supplies at very competitive prices, usually at sites outside the central shopping areas.

The growth of DIY has rejuvenated F. W. Woolworth, for example, for although its high-street operations have been declining, its DIY stores, B & Q, have become very profitable. Other increasingly familiar names are W. H. Smith's Do It All, Payless D.I.Y., Homebase and Texas Homecare.

Dogs. Brands with low market shares in low growth markets whose profitability prospects are dim. (See GROWTH/SHARE MATRIX.)

Down market. See UP MARKET.

Dumping. Offering goods for sale in foreign markets at lower prices than those prevailing in the domestic market. It is *prima facie* evidence of unfair competition and against the rules of the GENERAL AGREEMENT ON TARIFFS AND TRADE. Proving that dumping is taking place, however, is often difficult, due to exchange-rate fluctuations and the use of transfer pricing methods that may themselves be quite legitimate.

Durable goods. Goods that are not consumed and are expected to last over a period of time, such as refrigerators and washing machines (also known as WHITE GOODS), cars, clothing, computers and all types of machinery.

E

Early adopters. See DIFFUSION OF INNOVATION.

Electronic Funds Transfer at Point of Sale (EFTPOS). A technological development which enables the consumer to pay for goods at retail store checkout points with a plastic card which directly debits his bank account, eliminating the need to produce cash or write cheques/checks. The EFTPOS system is being tried experimentally, but it is thought that it will soon be in widespread use.

Electronic Point of Sale (EPOS). Checkout counters electronically equipped to read coded information, primarily the BAR CODE. Codes printed on each package are passed over an electronic scanner in the counter or read by using a hand-held electronic light pen. The information is fed into the store's computer where it is used to maintain up-to-the-minute inventory control. It may also be used to print out a fully itemized receipt for the customer.

Environmental scanning. The systematic examination of the business environment by marketing planners in order to identify marketing opportunities and threats. The business environment includes competitors, the domestic and international economy, social and cultural trends and technology. (See PLANNING.)

European Society for Opinion and Marketing Research (ESOMAR). The European equivalent of the MARKET RESEARCH SOCIETY (UK). Its annual conference is an important gathering for European researchers. Its Code of Practice sets standards for the conduct of European marketing research, covering responsibilities to informants, to clients, to field workers (interviewers) and to the profession.

Exchange. A transaction by which goods, services or money are traded for some other goods, services or money. Exchange is the central concept in MARKETING, as long as it is voluntary. The expected result of exchange is that benefit will accrue to both parties.

Exclusive dealing. A form of EXCLUSIVE DISTRIBUTION whereby a manufacturer grants a retailer the exclusive right to sell his products within a certain territory, on the condition that the retailer handles no directly competing products. It is a practice which may be interpreted as a restraint on free competition, and in the USA it has fallen foul of the Clayton Act. If it can be shown in a particular case that competition has been lessened or that a (local) monopoly has been created, the practice will be judged illegal. See RESALE PRICE MAINTENANCE.

Exclusive distribution. The right given by a manufacturer to a retailer to be the sole seller of the manufacturer's products in a given geographical area (a territory). Similar in many ways to FRANCHISING, it is a means of giving the manufacturer greater control over the distribution network, especially in respect to retail prices and services offered on the product. Business computers, high-quality luggage and fine china are normally sold on an exclusive distribution basis. (See EXCLUSIVE DEALING.)

Export Credits Guarantee Department (ECGD). A department of the British Government which provides exporters with insurance against major financial risks under the ECG scheme. Rates are set according to the products being exported and their destination.

Extended guarantees. Service and maintenance cover which a manufacturer offers for sale to a customer for a specified period of time beyond the term of the original guarantee. It is a kind of insurance policy against breakdown. (See WARRANTY.)

F

Fact book. A file of information about a product's history. It typically contains data on the product's sales, distribution and competition, its CUSTOMER PROFILE, any relevant market research findings, and a detailed record of the product's performance over time in relation to the marketing effort made on its behalf. Fact books are kept by company brand managers and advertising agency ACCOUNT MANAGERS.

Fads. A FASHION that is taken up with great enthusiasm, characterized by rapid sales growth and equally rapid decline: for example, the hoola hoop, the Rubic cube and the skateboard. (see PRODUCT LIFE CYCLE.)

Family brand. The use of one name, usually the company name, as part of the brand names of all the products in the company's PRODUCT LINE. (See BRAND.)

Family life cycle. A description of the stages of family life based on DEMOGRAPHIC data. It has been useful in defining the demand for certain goods and services, since each stage in the family life cycle produces distinguishable needs and interests (see MARKET SEGMENTATION). The seven stages in the cycle are: (1) young single people, (2) young couples with no children, (3) young couples with youngest child under six years, (4) couples with dependent children, (5) older couples with no children at home, and (6) older single people.

Fashion. A word used in marketing to describe a type of sales cycle seen in markets where style is important. The stages of the fashion cycle are distinctiveness, emulation, mass fashion and decline and are best illustrated by women's clothing fashions, which start in the haute couture salons of Paris, London and New York, are quickly imitated by mass manufacturers to eventually appear in the high-street clothing chain stores before they disappear in preparation for the next wave of fashion.

The term is not a precise one, however. It is often used to describe the prevailing practice not only in dress but in taste, manners, behaviour. Fashions may last for years or for 'a season'. Very short-lived fashions may be indistinguishable from FADS.

Fast food. The fastest-growing innovation in retailing in both the

UK and the USA. Although there had been hamburger joints, pizza parlours and especially fish and chip shops in the world before 1952, there was no 'fast food' until the McDonald Company raised its golden arches and invented it. Fast food means limited and standardized menus and self service coupled with friendly personnel, clean bright premises and reliable quality. Fast-food franchises have become commonplace on both sides of the Atlantic and continue to grow; there are more than 340 fast food chains in the USA and 60,000 outlets. The pioneering hamburger has been followed by pizza, chicken, tacoes, doughnuts, pastries, croissants, and even fish and chips (Arthur Treacher in the USA).

Fast-moving consumer goods (FMCGs). The name given to the kinds of products normally sold in SUPERMARKETS and SUPERSTORES, those which move off the shelves quickly and which require in-store inventories to be replenished constantly.

Father Christmas/Santa Claus. The paternal provider of gifts on Christmas Day, now more commonly arriving about the first of November as the harbinger of the Christmas retail sales drive!

Federal Trade Commission (FTC). The most important of a number of USA federal agencies that can have a major impact on marketing activity. The brief of the FTC is to ensure that trade practices are not deceptive nor unfair. It has broad powers over advertising claims and disclosures of product intent appearing on packages, including the power to require corrective advertising, at the advertiser's expense, when it is proved false or misleading claims have been made. (See NATIONAL ADVERTISING REVIEW BOARD.)

Flash pack. A package on which a SALES PROMOTION message is printed prominently, usually a price reduction. Products in flash packs are usually offered in limited quantities and for limited periods of time. Because precise quantities of the product are involved, the sales promotion costs can be exactly calculated.

Focus group interview. See GROUP DISCUSSION.

Franchising. A contractual agreement in which one party (the franchiser) sells the right to market goods or services to another party (the franchisee). McDonalds and Kentucky Fried Chicken are examples of successful retail franchising, the fastest-growing form of retailing in America and gaining in popularity in Britain. Franchising can also take place at wholesale level. Both Coca Cola and Pepsi Cola franchise their secret ingredients to wholesale bottlers who then produce and bottle the beverages and distribute them to retailers. An old and familiar franchising arrangement exists in the motor trade, where each dealer has an agreement with an automobile manufacturer. In retail franchising the franchiser provides the franchisee with a large number of marketing services in return for which the franchisee purchases equipment and supplies, pays franchising fees (often a large initial fee) and, frequently, a percentage of revenues.

The franchisee is usually given exclusive selling rights in a particular area.

Free lunch. Popularly believed to be an important marketing activity.

Freesheets. Giveaway newspapers or magazines. Because giveaway newspapers are supported exclusively by revenue from advertising, their circulation must be high and their costs low if they are to be profitable. They are circulated on a geographical basis (town, neighbourhood, suburb). Free magazines, on the other hand, such as airline or credit-card company magazines, though they carry advertising, are usually distributed selectively and may be subsidized by their sponsors for public relations purposes.

Frequency. The number of times an average person in a target audience is to be exposed to a MEDIA ADVERTISING message over a given period of time. Frequency is also known as 'opportunities to see' or 'OTSs'. (See MEDIA PLANNING.)

Functionalism. An approach to the study of marketing associated with the late Wroe Alderson and Ed McGarry, which led to the formalization of marketing as a subject for study. The functionalists moved away from the study of commodities and marketing institutions to the study of the functions of marketing, defined by McGarry as:

Contactual – the searching out of buyers and sellers;

Merchandising – the fitting of the goods to market requirements;

Pricing – the selection of a price high enough to make production possible and low enough to induce users to accept the goods;

Propaganda – the conditioning of buyers or sellers to a favourable attitude toward the product or its sponsor;

Physical distribution – the transporting and storing of the goods;

Termination – the consummation of the marketing process.

Modern MARKETING MANAGEMENT is a development of functionalism.

G

Gap analysis. A procedure for discerning marketing opportunities represented by gaps in the market, such as a neglected consumer group, a deficiency in existing product offerings, or an area suitable for exploitation because of some new technological development. Market researchers have developed sophisticated techniques for conducting gap analysis (see PERCEPTUAL MAPPING).

General Agreement on Tariffs and Trade (GATT). GATT is a club consisting of 70 of the world's leading trading countries, who meet every four years to consider international trade problems. Set up after World War II to deal with the then prevailing high tariff barriers, it negotiated reductions in their levels using the principle of most favoured nation (MFN). MFN works simply. If two members of GATT negotiate tariff reductions between themselves, then all members of GATT must enjoy the same reduced tariffs; in other words, all nations are subject to the lowest rate of tariff prevailing among members.

GATT has been a remarkably successful institution in postwar trade history, at least in respect to tariffs. It has not been so successful in reducing non-tariff barriers, such as quotas, restrictive customs practices, restrictive technical regulations, etc., however, nor has it greatly helped the Third World. The United Nations set up its own trade body, the United Nations Conference on Trade and Development (UNCTAD), as a bargaining agent.

General Electric Business Screen. A product PORTFOLIO ANALYSIS that overcomes some of the limitations of the GROWTH/SHARE MATRIX. The screen is more complex, having nine rather than four cells, and considers factors such as ease of competitive entry, production efficiency, market attractiveness, and investment alternatives (see opposite). Developed jointly by McKinsey and General Electric (USA), it is a sophisticated tool for developing product portfolio strategies.

Generic name. The name of a class or category of products, such as computers or soups. Sometimes the name of a successful BRAND comes to be used as a generic name: for example, Frigidaire to mean refrigerators (USA), Tide to mean detergents and

McKinsey General Electric Business Screen

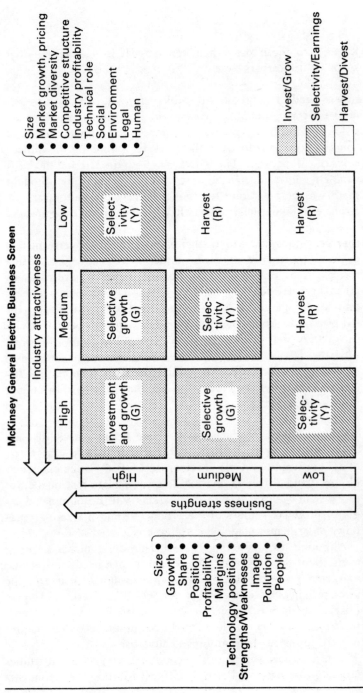

Source: McKinsey & Co. Reproduced with permission.

55

Kleenex to mean paper handkerchiefs. It is 'Hoovering' that keeps British carpets clean.

Generic need. The broadest possible definition of a market. The need for transportation, for example, is a generic need met by airlines, ships, buses, trains, cars, bicycles, etc. It is an important concept because it focusses the marketer's mind on the dimensions of competition. The railways in both the UK and the USA have gone into a decline because the railway companies thought there was no substitute for trains. Clearly the motor car, the airplane and the truck and lorry have demonstrated the contrary.

Generics. Goods sold with neither brand name nor advertising and promotion, usually in plain, undecorated packaging. Often referred to as Brand X goods, generics represent a response to criticism, particularly in the USA, that too much money is spent on marketing and that 'no frills' products will result in substantial price reductions. Generics have made inroads particularly in the grocery and pharmaceutical markets.

Gin and tonic brigade. An unkind term for members of the PUBLIC RELATIONS profession. In fact their drinking habits are much more eclectic.

Global products. Products which have brand names that are universally recognized. Not all of the world, but a very large part of it, knows Coca Cola, McDonald's, IBM, Guinness, Levi, Hilton, Land Rover. Some marketers speculate that in the not too distant future the world's markets will be dominated by global products because of the productive and marketing capability of large multinational corporations.

Although the marketing of global products makes assumptions about the universality of certain human needs and wants, marketers recognize that global BRANDS cannot be marketed the same way in every country. Procter & Gamble markets Pampers (disposable diapers/nappies) in 70 countries, but in each country the MARKETING MIX is tailored to the requirements of the market, in terms of price, distribution and advertising.

Brand names sometimes encounter unexpected difficulties crossing international borders. General Motors discovered that the Vauxhall Nova, which was acceptable in the UK, was not being received enthusiastically in Spain and Portugal: Nova in Spanish sounds like no va, 'no go'. With a name change to the Opel Corsa, sales improved.

Government publications. Governments publish data of great interest to marketers. In the UK, these include: BUSINESS MONITOR, *Monthly Digest* and *Annual Abstract of Statistics, Social Trends, Regional Trends, Family Expenditure, Household Food Consumption and Expenditure, General Household Survey*, and *Economic Trends and Overseas Trade Statistics*.

The government in the USA, both at federal and at state level, publishes data on almost every conceivable subject. Of particular interest to marketers are: *The Statistical Abstract of the US, County and City Data Bank, US Industrial Outlook, Market Information Guide, Census of Manufacturers, Census of Retail Trade, Wholesale Trade and Selected Service Industries, Survey of Current Business*, and *Vital Statistics Report*.

Grocery market shares. The power of the major retail chains in the grocery market is dramatically illustrated by the following data. In the UK, eight retail chains now account for 47.5 per cent of grocery shop sales and the trend suggests that concentrations will continue (see Table 9). In Table 10 it can be seen that small retailers (including small chains) are losing out to their larger competitors.

Table 9   *Grocery market shares 1984 (per cent of total grocery shop sales)*

Sainsbury	10.6
Tesco	10.2
Asda	6.1
Dee	5.5
Argyll	4.9
Fine Fare	4.3
Safeway	3.4
Kwik Save	2.5
Others	52.5

Source: The Times, 28 August 1985 (Euromonitor Publications).

Table 10 *Food distribution by outlet (per cent of food sales)*

	1980	1984
Hypermarkets and superstores	8	12
Supermarkets	28	33
Co-operatives	10	8
Department and variety stores	6	8
Others including small chains	48	39

Source: The Times, 28 August 1985 (Euromonitor Publications).

Group discussion. Informal, unstructured, personal interviews conducted in groups for MARKETING RESEARCH purposes. The interviewer has a list of topics to cover, but questionnaires are not used. The interaction of the group encourages wide-ranging exploration of a subject, making it a useful technique in many different areas of marketing research. Group discussion is typically used in NEW PRODUCT DEVELOPMENT to test ideas and products and by ADVERTISING AGENCIES in copy testing.

It is one of the chief tools for QUALITATIVE RESEARCH. (See DEPTH INTERVIEW.)

Also known as focus group interview.

Growth/share matrix. The technique associated with the name of the Boston Consulting Group (hence popularly called 'the Boston Box') used for analysing a company's portfolio of businesses (SBUs) or products. The growth/share matrix focusses on each product's position in the PRODUCT LIFE CYCLE (its market growth rate) and its competitive strength (its market share), with cash generation being of critical interest. The matrix has four cells representing high market share products in low growth markets ('CASH COWS'), high market share products in high growth markets ('STARS'), low market share products in high growth markets ('PROBLEM CHILDREN') and low market share products in low growth markets ('DOGS').

Cash cows, because they require relatively low levels of marketing investment and benefit from cost savings associated with high output, marketing skill and experience, are generators of cash. They are not candidates for expansion but are quietly maintained and tended for their flow of cash. Well-known cash cows are Corn Flakes for Kellogg's, Nescafe for Nestles, Bovril

The growth/share matrix

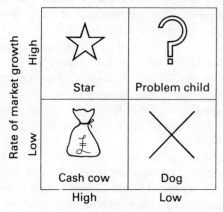

Rate of market growth: High / Low

Star — Problem child

Cash cow — Dog

Relative market share: High / Low

Growth/share matrix – cash value

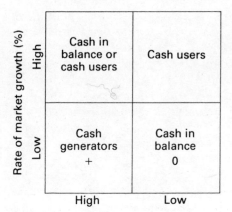

Rate of market growth (%): High / Low

Cash in balance or cash users	Cash users
Cash generators +	Cash in balance 0

Relative market share: High / Low

for Beechams, Dairy Milk Chocolate for Cadbury's, and Miller High Life Beer for Philip Morris.

Stars are potential cash cows but need substantial expenditures of cash on advertising, distribution, etc., to ensure they maintain their market share until the market matures.

Problem children may succeed or fail. If it is decided they may have a profitable future, they too will require very heavy expenditure of cash to enable them to increase their market share. If not, they may quickly become dogs.

Dogs have small prospect of future growth or increased market share and so are candidates for deletion from the company's portfolio of products.

The growth/share matrix was developed in the 1970s and had a dramatic impact on the way companies viewed their PRODUCT MIX. PORTFOLIO ANALYSIS is now an essential tool in the development of MARKETING STRATEGY, but other techniques have been developed which take into account more factors than simply market share and market growth rate (see GENERAL ELECTRIC BUSINESS SCREEN and DIRECTIONAL POLICY MATRIX).

H

Habit. Buying behaviour in which a consumer buys the same BRAND again and again. Habit buying implies the absence of dissatisfaction with a brand rather than positive loyalty to it and is usually associated with the purchase of LOW-INVOLVEMENT PRODUCTS. It is often possible to sway habit buyers from their habitual brands by SALES PROMOTIONS.

Hall tests. MARKETING RESEARCH tests conducted in some place (a room or hall) located conveniently near a shopping centre. Shoppers are selected by researchers and invited to come to the 'hall' to participate in the tests. Commonly used for PRODUCT TESTING and for PRE-TESTING advertising, price, BRAND names and PACKAGING. (See VAN TESTS.)

Harvesting strategy. The reaping of short-term profit from a product prior to withdrawing it from the market. If it is judged that a product is coming to the end of its PRODUCT LIFE CYCLE, marketing expenditures on it will be reduced; typically, advertising will be withdrawn. Because the effects of earlier advertising will still be felt, the product will continue to sell, producing attractive net profits during its last days.

For some products, last days can draw out into years if large enough bands of die-hard customers exist. Ipana toothpaste and Lifebuoy soap both lived profitably on years after marketing support had been withdrawn.

Hawkers. Intinerant door-to-door salesmen. Public response to this type of retailing may be inferred from the notices once commonly attached to garden gates: 'No hawkers, no circulars'.

Heavy users. A very important dimension of MARKET SEGMENTATION, since usage rates are critically important in some product fields. In the USA, research done some years ago (1964) revealed the following statistics:

> 39% of all families consumed 90% of all cola drinks.
> 48% of all families consumed 87% of all ready-to-eat cereals.
> 16% of all households consumed 88% of all beer (66% of all households consumed no beer at all).

A survey done in the UK in 1985 showed that:

> 61% of all petrol was bought by 19% of men.

65% of all lager was bought by 9% of men.
66% of all ground coffee was bought by 8% of women.
80% of all fabric conditioner was bought by 9% of women.
73% of all gin was bought by 5% of adults.

Clearly marketers try to direct their efforts towards the segment of the market that accounts for the heaviest use of their product. Shaefer beer (USA) was advertised as the 'One beer to have when you're having more than one'. Heineken observed that they would use the medium of direct mail to advertise to the 9 per cent of men who drink 65 per cent of all the lager – if only there were a means of getting their names and addresses!

Hierarchy of effects. The steps in the persuasion process leading to a purchase decision. The hierarchy moves from awareness to knowledge to liking to preference to conviction to purchase. Marketing communications are constructed with the hierarchy in mind and salespersons will often follow the steps in the hierarchy in making a sales presentation. (See AIDA and ADVERTISING.)

High-involvement products. Products over which consumers take time and trouble (shopping around, price comparisons, financing arrangements) in reaching a purchase decision, because factors of self image, cost and product performance are involved. Cars, homes, fitted kitchens, hi-fi systems and package tour holidays are examples of high-involvement products.

Home audits. MARKETING RESEARCH conducted in the home by marketing research companies using DIARY PANELS to record on some regular basis (weekly, monthly, etc.) what products householders buy and how often they buy them.

Hype. Exaggeration for effect is the meaning of the word 'hyperbole'. Characteristically, the inventors of marketing jargon have shortened the word and made it part of the language. All 'over-the-top' marketing events and announcements are examples of marketing hype.

Hypermarket. A French invention, the word being the anglicized version of *hypermarché* ('supermarket'). Carrefours is a French hypermarket chain with stores located in the UK. (See SUPER-STORES.)

I

Image. The picture or feeling or association which the name of a brand (store or company) calls up in a person's mind. A product's image is what that product means to a person. Maytag washing machines (USA) mean 'reliability' – 'Maytags don't break down'. Volvo motor cars mean 'safety'. Jaguar means 'class'.

In recent years advertising has paid less attention to communicating product attributes (see UNIQUE SELLING PROPOSITION) and has concentrated instead on creating strong product image. (See POSITIONING.)

"I hear she's had media lessons back home."

Impulse buying. Spur of the moment decisions to buy, made at the time of purchase. Goods which are apt to be bought impulsively (magazines, candy/sweets, gum) are usually placed close to the point of payment. Goods which are often bought routinely, like cereals or shampoos, may also be subject to impulse buying: one's regular brand may be passed over if another catches the eye or is the focus of a SALES PROMOTION.

Incorporated Society of British Advertisers Ltd (ISBA). Founded in 1900 as the Advertisers Protection Society, the Society is open to any advertising company and is concerned with all matters relating to ADVERTISING.

Independents. Individually owned retail shops which do not belong to, and are therefore 'independent' of, a corporate chain. In most lines of retailing, independents have been losing business to the corporate chains; in grocery retailing, for example, their share of total turnover has declined continuously over the past 20 years (see GROCERY MARKET SHARES). One way independents have tried to maintain their viability is by joining a VOLUNTARY CHAIN.

The term is also applied to small manufacturing companies in an industry dominated by relatively few large manufacturers. Thus in the oil industry, a few independents maintain a rather precarious existence in a world dominated by less than a dozen major oil companies.

Independent Broadcasting Authority (IBA). In the UK, the IBA watches over standards of commercial television, through application of the IBA Code of Practice. The Code is quite elaborate, but Section 12 sets its tone: no advertisement should offend against good taste or decency or be offensive to public feeling. All commercials have to be vetted/previewed by the IBA before screening, in contrast with the practice of the ADVERTISING STANDARDS AUTHORITY.

The Code does not allow religious or political advertising and has very strict rules for charity and family planning advertisements – so strict that such advertising rarely appears. It is also demanding with respect to advertisements of financial services and medicines and advertisements directed at children. Cigarette advertising is banned. Beer and light spirits may be advertised, but hard liquor such as whisky may not. Furthermore, no one appearing in alcoholic drink commercials can appear to be younger than 25. Advertisements must not *without justifiable reason* play on fear – a clause that has allowed powerful road-safety advertisements.

A recent relaxation in the Code has allowed 'knocking copy', commercials that compare named rival brands with the advertiser's brand, but all technical claims made in the comparisons have to be checked.

Industrial Marketing Research Association (IMRA). The professional association for people engaged in research into the marketing of goods and services to corporate and institutional users. The growth of research into such markets and its distinctive nature compared with that for consumer goods led to the formation of the Association in 1963, since when it has become the recognized national body representing professional industrial marketing research in the UK.

Inertia selling. A form of selling familiar to anyone who has ever belonged to a book club. If you do not cancel the monthly selection, you receive the book! The sale is made as a result of inertia or the customer's failure to take any action to stop it.

Innovation. The process of developing and introducing new products or new product designs into the market. Under pressure of competition, companies try to preserve their COMPETITIVE ADVANTAGE by continuous product innovation. As the rate of innovation increases, the time a product has to produce a profit for the company is reduced, putting more pressure on the company to innovate. The successful management of the process of innovation, therefore, is crucial to most firms' success. Some companies concentrate their efforts on bringing out products based on established market demand, a new detergent, for example, or a new line of cosmetics. Other companies are true innovators, developing technological firsts, like the home computer or the compact disc player.

Innovators. Consumers who are the first to try and to use a new product, typically only a small percentage of the population.

Research suggests that innovators tend to be people who are well educated, well informed, well to do, open minded, upwardly mobile, and reachable by the mass MEDIA. The same people will not be innovators for every product. A new method of seed drilling will appeal to one group of innovators while compact disc players will appeal to another. But marketers will always try to identify the innovator group for any given product and concentrate their efforts there. (See DIFFUSION OF INNOVATION.)

Institute of Export (IE). A body representing the interests of exporting companies. It is a useful source of international trade data, runs training courses for exporters (the Diploma of the Institute) and lays particular stress on the management of planning, shipping, delivery and service as components of the 'total export concept'.

Institute of Marketing (IM). The professional body representing marketing managers in the UK. Founded in 1911, its current membership is over 20,000 full members and 16,000 student members throughout the world. Its objectives are 'to develop knowledge about marketing, to provide services for members and registered students and to make the principles and practices of marketing more widely known and used throughout industry and commerce'.

The Institute engages in a wide range of activities. As part of its involvement with business, it runs a Marketing Advisory Service, offers annual awards to companies which have successfully applied marketing techniques (increased profits), and acts as the spokesman for marketing managers. It plays an important role in marketing education, providing Certificate and Diploma courses in Marketing at institutions around the country, as well as supporting an extensive programme of training courses at its headquarters, Moor Hall, in Cookham. The Institute publishes a weekly magazine, *Marketing*, and the *Quarterly Review of Marketing*.

Institute of Packaging (IP). A professional body founded in 1947 devoted to catering for the needs of packaging technologists and managers.

Institute of Practitioners in Advertising (IPA). The professional organization for UK advertising agencies, established in 1917. Between 85 and 95 per cent of all advertising placed by UK agencies is handled by its members. It conducts education and training courses in ADVERTISING for its members.

Institute of Public Relations (IPR). Founded in 1948, the only professional public relations organization in the UK and the largest in Europe.

Institute of Purchasing and Supply (IPS). The professional institute of buyers and sellers of industrial goods, dedicated to raising professional standards through education and training of those employed in the purchasing and supply functions of both business and government.

Institute of Sales Promotion (ISP). The professional body of the branch of marketing known as SALES PROMOTION. The purpose of the organization is to raise the status and appreciation of the role of sales promotion in the UK and in Europe. Although the sales promotion industry has had a professional body since 1933, the Institute came into being in 1978 as a result of the reorganization of an earlier body, the Sales Promotion Executives Association (1969).

Institutional advertising. Though most ADVERTISING is concerned with products and services, many organizations advertise themselves. Companies whose brands are conspicuously linked with the company name, such as DuPont or General Electric (USA) and Zanussi (UK), expect corporate advertising to create favourable public attitudes toward the company which will carry over to the company's brands.

Companies whose operations may provoke public hostility, such as oil, mining, chemical or nuclear power companies, try to counter negative attitudes. Chevron Oil in the USA, for example, advertises the fact that it is preserving the habitat of a tiny endangered species of butterfly in the midst of its giant refinery next to the huge Los Angeles International Airport. In the UK, Shell advertising pictures a beautiful Welsh valley, asking the viewer what he would do to protect that valley against the ravages of a bulldozer carving out a way for a pipeline. Shell then says what it would be prepared to do, revealing that it has already laid the pipeline and restored the valley to the condition the viewer sees.

Giant multinational companies whose portfolios include a wide range of businesses may also advertise in order to establish a name people will be familiar with. United Technologies (USA) has run a series of advertisements in top newspapers and magazines which feature homilies on profound but non-controversial subjects. Only the name of the company appears at the bottom of the page, no mention of any product, but the series has proved very popular, eliciting thousands of requests for reprints.

Intention to buy. Attempts are sometimes made to forecast sales on the basis of consumers' intentions to buy. Research is carried out, particularly in the field of industrial goods, to ascertain such 'intentions'. Since the respondent has little to lose by his answers, it is not considered a very sound basis for SALES FORECASTING.

Interactive marketing. The MARKETING MIX describes the responsibilities of marketing managers. As a model of marketing it has been criticized as being too deterministic: it suggests that suppliers have total control over the marketing process and that customers are passive. Interactive marketing is an approach that stresses that both buyers and sellers are active in decision-making, that success is dependent upon the competence and ability of individuals and organizations involved in the interaction process, and that an understanding of the relationships and interdependence between supplier and customer is essential to the marketing process. An equally important dimension of interaction is the atmosphere surrounding the relationship, the degree of co-operation and conflict and overall social distance between buyers and sellers.

Interactive marketing describes most industrial markets, particularly where customers specify the nature of the products they wish to purchase. It is useful in understanding the nature of INTERNATIONAL MARKETING where different cultures complicate relationships between buyers and sellers. Interactive marketing is also relevant to consumer markets since the nature of many consumer markets can be understood only by analysing the relationships between manufacturers (suppliers) and the distribution system. Retail networks dominated by large MULTIPLES exercise extensive control over what they stock, specifying products and often requiring that these products carry the retailer's brand name. Marketing to these networks is an interactive process. (See DEALER BRAND, GROCERY MARKET SHARE and RETAILERS.)

International marketing. Products, brands and some retail outlets are becoming increasingly familiar worldwide. Some brands are so familiar that consumers assume they must be marketed by indigenous companies. The nationalities of the brands featured in Table 11 may provide some surprises.

Though most Britons know that McDonald's and Kentucky Fried Chicken are American, there are probably few Americans

Table 11 *Nationality of various brands*

Home country	Brand	Company
UK/Netherlands	Vim, Persil	Unilever
	Signal toothpaste	(Lever Bros)
	Lux soap	
	Shell oil & petroleum products	Shell
Netherlands	Philips electrical products	Philips
UK	Aquafresh toothpaste	Beecham Group
	Macleans toothpaste	
	Kiwi shoe polish	Reckitts
USA	Tide detergent	Procter & Gamble
	Head & Shoulders shampoo	
	Crest toothpaste	
	Maxwell House coffee	General Foods
	Heinz baked beans, etc.	Heinz
	Woolworth's stores	Woolworth
Switzerland	Nescafé coffee	Nestlé
	Swatch watches	Asuag

aware that Saks Fifth Avenue, Gimbels, Baskin and Robbins, and until very recently Howard Johnson's, are British owned. The web of international products, markets and channels of distribution is becoming increasingly elaborate.

Interviewer Card Scheme (ICS). A system that provides marketing researchers in the UK with identification credentials. Many people who are stopped in the street by researchers are hesitant and suspicious that someone might be trying to sell them something. The ICS, sponsored and administered by the MARKET RESEARCH SOCIETY, provides an identification card to each interviewer who belongs to a company approved by the Society. Its objectives are:

1 to protect the general public by providing a safeguard against abuse of the personal interview situation;
2 to uphold and support the Code of Conduct of the Market Research Society;
3 to promote the Interviewer Card Scheme among the interviewers, buyers, and users of research; and
4 to keep in mind the interests of the whole industry.

Invisible account. The quaint British term for export trade that deals in intangibles, primarily the provision of services. It includes shipping, air freight, tourism, insurance and international banking. Far from being invisible in its effect, the UK invisible account in most years shows a favourable balance of trade.

"Good morning, madam. Could you spare a moment? This time we're conducting a survey to discover how many pople would stop to talk to a market researcher dressed as a pig."

J

Joint Industry Committee for National Readership Surveys (JICNARS). Reports twice yearly on the reading habits of 28,000 individuals, covering over 200 national newspapers and magazines. The National Readership Survey has been continuous since 1956; JICNARS was formed in 1968 to run the surveys. It is also an important source of information on matters other than reading habits. Because it uses a large random sample, it provides insights into social grade distribution (see SOCIAL GRADING) and household composition.

Joint Industry Committee for Poster Audience Surveys (JICPAS). Represents advertisers, ADVERTISING AGENCIES and associations of poster (billboard) site owners in the UK. The Committee supervises the collection of data on OPPORTUNITIES TO SEE poster sites, enabling advertisers to compare the cost effectiveness of poster sites compared with other advertising MEDIA.

Joint Industry Committee for Radio Audience Research (JICRAR). Provides information about the listening habits of radio audiences, particularly those tuned to commercial stations.

Judgement sampling. In survey research, the selection of respondents for a sample based on criteria judged by the researcher to be most appropriate for the purposes of the research. Judgement sampling is most frequently used in industrial marketing research. In an industry dominated by a few manufacturers, the researcher may decide that a sample representative of those few is more significant than a sample of all the industry's manufacturers. (See NON-PROBABILITY SAMPLING.)

Junk mail. A term for promotional and advertising material of all kinds that arrives, unsolicited, in the morning's mail. The judgement which the term implies is picturesque but not entirely accurate. (See DIRECT MAIL.)

"What I miss most about being of no fixed address is junk mail."

L

Le marketing. What did the French do before *le media planning, le marketing mix, le merchandizing, le packaging, le couponing, l'interview, le cash and carry, le consumerism, le self-service, le jingle, le fast food, le push-pull, le Cornflakes* and *le ketchup* enabled them to engage in *le marketing*?

Learning. Consumers learn from experience. All MODELS of buyer behaviour incorporate the notion that learning takes place and that each decision to purchase is heavily influenced by experience gained from previous purchases.

Leasing. A contractual arrangement in which the use of a piece of equipment over a period of time is sold by one party (the lessor) to another party (the lessee). Leasing rather than outright purchase is attractive to some companies because it reduces cash flow in the short term (no capital outlay) and may also guarantee service, important in the case of complicated equipment. It also offers the prospect of updating products on favourable terms. Firms leasing computers or company cars, for example, have exploited this marketing opportunity.

Licensing. Selling the right to use some process, trademark, patent, etc., on a fee or royalty basis. It is a relatively low-risk way to enter a foreign market, since the licensee (the purchaser of the right) bears most of the risks incurred. If the licensee is an effective marketer, the licenser (the seller of the right) may reap a good reward.

Licensing is often used to enter markets where direct entry is difficult, for example Japan or Eastern Europe. Gerber, for example, markets baby food in Japan through a licensing agreement; Corning Glass licenses the right to manufacture television tubes to a Yugoslav state corporation; and Massey-Ferguson-Perkins Ltd licenses Agromet-Motoimport of Poland to manufacture tractors.

Lifestyle. The way a person chooses to live, based on his attitudes toward life. Segmenting markets (see MARKET SEGMENTATION) by life style is popular among market researchers trying to classify groups of consumers in ways that relate to purchase behaviour. One such classification, developed by the Stanford Research

Institute in the USA, is Values and Life Styles (VALS) (see John O'Shaughnessy, *Competitive Marketing* (Allen & Unwin, 1984).

Belongers: patriotic, stable, sentimental traditionalists who are content with their lives.

Achievers: prosperous, self-assured middle-aged materialists.

Emulators: ambitious young adults trying to break into the system.

I-am-me group: impulsive, experimental, a bit narcissistic.

Societally conscious: mature, successful, mission-oriented people who like causes.

Survivors: the old and poor with little optimism about the future.

Sustainers: resentful of their condition in trying to make ends meet.

(See FAMILY LIFE CYCLE and PSYCHOGRAPHICS.)

Line extending. Increasing a PRODUCT LINE by adding variations of an existing BRAND. When a company has a successful brand, there is a temptation to use the brand name on other products. Thus a well-known brand of hand lotion might have variants for dry skin, sensitive skin, detergent damaged skin, and so on. Line extending runs the risk of weakening the brand name.

Line filling. Adding more products to an existing PRODUCT LINE in order to leave no gaps into which competitors might move. Procter & Gamble, masters at this activity, have fourteen BRANDS of detergent (Ivory Snow, Dreft, Tide, Joy, Cheer, Oxydol, Dash, Cascade, Duz, Ivory Liquid, Gain, Dawn, Era, and Bold), each differentiated in some way from the others.

When product lines are increased by moving UP or DOWN MARKET to attract new customers, the process is sometimes called line stretching. In the office copier market the major manufacturers have stretched the line both upwards (large, multifunctional machines, high speed with sorting capability) and downward (small machines low enough in price that some are purchased for use in the home). Each copier is different enough from the others in the line to make differentiation on grounds other than price possible. (See MULTI-BRAND STRATEGY.)

Line stretching. See LINE FILLING.

Loss-leader pricing. A retail pricing device, designed to attract customers into a shop. A product is offered for sale by the retailer at a low price (a loss), in the hope it will 'lead' customers into the shop where they will buy not only the low-priced item (the loss leader) but full-priced items as well. It is frequently done on a limited availability basis – 'to the first 25 customers only' or 'while the supply lasts'.

Loss-leader pricing is a device to promote the retail outlet rather than the product, and manufacturers are not always pleased to have their products so used. Martini & Rossi, for example, have withheld supplies from stores who use their products as loss leaders.

Low-involvement products. Products purchased without much deliberation and forethought. They do not involve egos nor very much money: a poor purchasing decision does not have important consequences. Marketers try to make their low-involvement products more interesting to consumers through ADVERTISING so that BRAND LOYALTY may develop (the Andrex toilet tissue puppy or Lux film stars).

M

Macro marketing. The term comes from the field of economics and refers to MARKETING studied in the context of large aggregations rather than small units (micro marketing). It is concerned with the flow of goods and services from producers to consumers as it occurs within economic systems and with the social processes which direct such flows. The study of marketing institutions and the functional approach to marketing (see FUNCTIONALISM) are also the domain of macro marketing. Micro marketing, in contrast, is concerned with marketing processes in individual companies and with consumers and organizational buyer behaviour.

Mail order. The use of the post office as a DISTRIBUTION CHANNEL, linking manufacturer, wholesaler and/or retailer directly with the consumer. Based on catalogue selling, Littlewoods (UK) and Sears Roebuck (USA) are long-established and successful mail-order businesses. It is a popular and growing type of retailing, attracting new entrants into the field. Service organizations such as American Express and Access (UK) have moved into mail-order selling as have Avon and General Foods in the USA. (See DIRECT MARKETING.)

Mail survey. MARKETING RESEARCH carried out by mail. Since respondents have time to reflect over the questionnaires before answering, this type of enquiry has advantages over telephone or personal interviews. Most mail surveys, however, suffer from low return rates, a disadvantage that adds cost to an otherwise low-cost operation if the respondents have to be followed up by telephone. Known as 'postal survey' in the UK.

Manufacturer brand. A BRAND created by a manufacturer, such as Kelloggs, Kodak, Esso, Ford. Sometimes known as a national brand. (See DEALER BRAND.)

Manufacturer's agent. An independent MIDDLEMAN who sells goods on behalf of one or more manufacturer. He may carry goods on consignment and provide services such as financing or installation. Agents sell to wholesalers, retailers or industrial buyers and are paid on commission.

Manufacturer's recommended price. Some manufacturers

attempt to control the price at which their products are sold at retail and accordingly issue a price list containing their recommendations. In the UK, prior to the Restrictive Trade Practices Act (1956), recommended price was closely observed (see RESALE PRICE MAINTENANCE). Today its only effect may be to provide retailers with a figure they can quote as a means of drawing attention to their own lower prices. The attractiveness to the retailer of this practice has occasionally resulted in the invention of manufacturers' recommended prices, should the manufacturers themselves have failed to produce them!

Manufacturer's sales branch. A wholesaling business owned by the manufacturer rather than a MIDDLEMAN, which provides showrooms, sales and service for the manufacturer's products. Sales branches are usually located in sales-rich locations, with the result that in the USA, although they make up only 11 per cent of wholesale businesses, they account for 36 per cent of total wholesale sales. Manufacturers of computers and domestic appliances typically have strategically placed sales branches.

Manufacturer's selling price. The price charged by manufacturers to their customers, who may be wholesalers, retailers, or end users. When QUANTITY DISCOUNTS are given (and they usually are), the manufacturer's selling price will not be the final price paid by the customer but the price upon which the discount is calculated.

Mark-up pricing. A pricing technique widely used by retailers whereby a product's selling price is set by adding a certain percentage to (by marking up) its cost price. This mark-up percentage is the profit margin taken by the retailer.

Market. In marketing usage, a group of consumers who share some particular characteristic which may affect their needs or wants are and who are potential buyers of a product. Examples are the soap market, the teenage market, the housing market, the leisure market, the American market.

Market and Opinion Research International (MORI). A UK MARKETING RESEARCH company engaged in a wide range of research activities but known best for its social and political research and its widely publicized MORI public opinion poll.

Market demand. The total volume of demand for a PRODUCT CLASS in a given time period. Each company must estimate the share of the total market demand it can expect to obtain, given the size of its marketing investment. That estimate, the sales potential figure, then becomes the basis of the company's SALES FORECAST.

Market Research Society (MRS). The professional body for individuals using survey techniques for market, social and economic research. More than 35 years old, it has about 5000 members and claims to be the largest organization of its kind in the world.

It publishes a *Newsletter* (monthly), the *Journal of the Market Research Society, Survey* (quarterly) and *Market Research Abstracts* (half-yearly).

Market segmentation. It is generally more satisfactory to market to groups of consumers who have similar characteristics, wants and needs than to the general undifferentiated public: the match between what the consumer wants and what the manufacturer offers is likely to be closer. These groups of consumers having something in common are called 'market segments' and the process of identifying them, 'market segmentation'.

Markets may be segmented in many different ways, depending on the insight or perceptiveness of the marketer. Consumer market segments are commonly based on the following kinds of characteristics:

DEMOGRAPHIC (e.g. age, sex, income, education). Sheltered housing targets the over-60's market, and Rolls Royce makes cars for the high-income market.

Geographic (e.g. country, state, region). A company may choose to sell its products in selected areas, or it may sell different products in different areas. Nestle markets Nescafe in both the USA and the UK, but its decaffeinated freeze-dried Taster's Choice is not distributed to the British market.

PSYCHOGRAPHIC (e.g. social class, LIFESTYLE, personality). Manufacturers of clothes, furniture, food products, cosmetics, drinks, cars give great attention to market segments based on these variables.

Use (e.g. occasion, BENEFIT looked for, user status, user rate). There is a hot drink before bedtime market, a summer barbecue market, a charter airflight market; a health food market, a GENERIC BRAND market. There are potential user, first time user and regular user markets and markets segmented into light, medium and heavy users. It is a fact of great interest to beer manufacturers that 88 per cent of all beer consumed in the USA is consumed by 18 per cent of all families in the USA. 65 per cent of all lager drunk in the UK is bought by 9 per cent of UK men.

Industrial markets are frequently segmented by type of organization (e.g. manufacturing, governmental, agricultural) or type of goods required (raw materials, installations, services).

A market segment must meet certain standards if it is to be the focus of a marketing effort. Its size and purchasing power must be substantial enough to promise a profitable return, it must be accessible, and it must have future as well as present viability.

Market share. A valuable measure of a company's marketing success. Market share is defined as a company's sales expressed as a percentage of total sales in a given MARKET. It is usually looked at in comparison with the market shares of competitors as an indication of competitive strength, and it is an essential ingredient in PORTFOLIO ANALYSIS.

Defining the boundaries of a market may present difficulties. Is market share for instant coffee calculated on the basis of all instant coffee sales, or all coffee sales, or all beverage sales? The extent of a company's strength or weakness, therefore, when measured by market share figures, depends very much on how the market is defined.

Market test. An attempt to test a new product's performance in the marketplace by test launching it in a limited area. Unlike product testing, market testing requires that the full intended national marketing strategy be simulated within the selected area. In the UK, many market tests take place in one of the ITV (commercial television) regional areas. Television ADVERTISING may then be fully exploited without breaching the limits of the test area. Full-scale market testing is expensive and carries no guarantees that the product will succeed nationally; although the practice has become less frequent in recent years, many consumer goods first appear under market-test conditions.

Marketing. Defined by the INSTITUTE OF MARKETING as 'the management process responsible for identifying, anticipating and satisfying customer requirements profitably'. Since non-profit organizations can also utilize the marketing process, the definition might be expanded to 'those activities performed by individuals or organizations, whether profit or non-profit, that enable, facilitate, and encourage exchange to take place to the satisfaction of both parties'. Emphasis on satisfying customer requirements is central to any definition of marketing. (See MARKETING CONCEPT and MARKETING MANAGEMENT.)

Marketing audit. The term 'marketing audit' has two not unrelated meanings. It is frequently applied to extensive PRODUCTIVITY analysis, a process that judges how well resources are being used in a company's marketing department. In this context the term is used in an 'accounting' sense, an investigation enabling the auditor to draw conclusions about the stewardship of the marketing management. It is a concept that is much better understood in America than in Britain.

The second meaning relates to the PLANNING process. One of the critical steps in that process is to assess the existing marketing situation and the company's marketing capability. This assessment is often called the marketing audit. (See SWOT ANALYSIS.)

Marketing Board. A quasi-governmental body with responsibility for the marketing of primarily agricultural products, where product differentiation between individual producers is difficult. Marketing Boards act on behalf of all producers, attempting to increase demand for the product. In some cases BRANDS may be used: Jaffa, for example, is the brand name used by the Citrus Marketing Board of Israel. In the UK, the Milk Marketing Board collects and distributes milk in bulk as well as marketing milk products through its subsidiary, Dairy Crest.

Marketing budget. A financial statement about the level of marketing effort to be undertaken by a company. The marketing budget represents the cost of achieving the company's marketing objectives and strategies as described in the MARKETING PLAN.

The budget is expressed as a profit and loss statement, showing both the revenues anticipated from sales and the costs of the marketing resources that will be put into the MARKETING MIX.

Budgets are made at each PLANNING level. At brand level, a typical budget might take the form of Table 12.

Table 12 *A typical budget at brand level*

	£	£	£
Revenue (forecast)			4,000,000
Advertising and sales			
Promotion costs		1,300,000	
Advertising	700,000		
Sales and distribution	300,000		
Consumer promotions	200,000		
Trade promotions	100,000		
Overhead allocations		230,000	
Research and development	150,000		
Marketing research	50,000		
Administration	30,000		
Manufacturing costs		1,200,000	
Fixed	400,000		
Variable	800,000		
Total costs		2,730,000	
Forecast profits before tax			1,270,000

Marketing channel. See DISTRIBUTION CHANNEL.

Marketing concept. The marketing concept expresses the role of marketing in contemporary society: marketing should be customer-oriented, providing customers with what they want and need. By contrast, the outmoded philosophy of product marketing orients a company toward the product, placing the burden of finding customers on an aggressive sales force.

The marketing concept requires that all company decision's should be based upon accurate knowledge of the company's customers, acquired through meticulous monitoring of the marketplace.

Marketing department. Although the size of a company will determine the way its marketing department is organized, the diagram on p. 84 shows one of the commonest forms of organization based on the marketing functions the company performs.

Marketing flops. About 80 per cent of all new products never become commercial successes. An enterprising Scot and chairman of Marketing Intelligence Service Ltd, Robert McMath, has opened a product museum in Naples, New York, where some of these failures have been saved from total oblivion. Touch of Yogurt shampoo, Gorilla Balls vitamin enriched malt candy, Nullo deodorant tablets, Male Chauvinist 'awfully arrogant aftershave' and 'outrageously superior cologne', Northwoods Egg Coffee and Baker Tom's Baked Cat Food are a few which represent pain and disappointment to unknown entrepreneurs.

But the mighty make mistakes, too, and their failures become famous. Ford offered its large powerful Edsel to a market that wanted small economy cars. Gerber correctly identified young adults as a market for quickly prepared food but misjudged what the young adults' response would be to adult food packed in baby food jars. They didn't buy it. Procter & Gamble was outwitted by the competition when it introduced its new product, Pringle Potato Chips (crisps), to the American market. It seemed headed for success until Wise Potato Chips advertised on television, 'In Wise, you find: Potatoes. Vegetable oil. Salt. In Pringle's you find: Dehydrated potatoes. Mono- and diglycerides. Ascorbic acid. Butylated hydroxy-anisole.' Pringle's never made it.

Marketing intelligence. The way corporate executives keep themselves informed about the changing market environment, using such means as ENVIRONMENTAL SCANNING. In the USA, marketing intelligence systems for generating such information are in common use. In the UK, companies have been slower to use MARKETING RESEARCH for this purpose. The term 'intelligence' in this context is used in the military sense – piecing together information to form a picture of the competition's potentialities and intentions.

Organization of a Marketing Department

President
or
Managing Director

- Director of Finance
- Director of Marketing
  - Advertising and Sales Promotion
  - Sales
  - Marketing Research
- Director of Research & Development
  - Product Planning
- Director of Production
  - Marketing Administration

> Before the war, he was an alert, hard hitting, aggressive marketing executive. As such, he was a very bad marketing executive. Colonel Cargill was so awful a marketing executive that his services were much sought after by firms eager to establish losses for tax purposes.
>
> Joseph Heller, *Catch 22*

Marketing management. One of the four major management divisions in a company, along with production management, finance management and research and development.

The COMMITTEE OF MARKETING ORGANIZATIONS (COMO) has identified nine responsibilities of marketing management:

1 Finding out the facts (MARKET RESEARCH).
2 Predictions arising from research (FORECASTING).
3 Changes arising from research (NEW PRODUCT DEVELOPMENT).
4 Will customers want to buy? (BRAND MANAGEMENT).
5 In what quantities? (Budgeting).
6 At what price? At what profit? (Pricing Policy).
7 Moving goods from point of manufacture to point of consumption or use (DISTRIBUTION).
8 Sales as part of marketing (SALES MANAGEMENT).
9 Persuasive communication (ADVERTISING).

Marketers summarize these responsibilities as the four Ps: product policy, pricing policy, placing policy, and promotion policy, to which should be added PLANNING and PRODUCTIVITY measurement. The following diagram illustrates the major marketing functions. (See MARKETING MIX.)

Major marketing functions

General marketing functions

1 Determining marketing objectives
2 Developing marketing plans
3 Budgeting sales, expenses, margins, profits
4 Coordinating marketing activities
5 Developing marketing executives

Marketing research	Product	Distribution	Sales force management	Advertising and sales promotion

Marketing mix. The areas of company decision making that should be under the supervision of the marketing manager, namely product policy (what product is going to be offered to the customer?), pricing policy (how much is the customer going to pay for the product?), promotional policy (how is the customer going to know about the product and be persuaded to buy it?), and distribution policy (how is the product going to be where the customer is when the customer wants it?). Table 13 shows the kinds of decisions appropriate to each of these areas.

The term 'marketing mix' is an apt description for the various elements of the marketing process that must be co-ordinated to make up the total marketing effort. These elements are known among marketers as the four Ps: product, price, place and promotion.

Table 13 *Components of the marketing mix*

Product	Characteristics
	Brand names
	Packaging
	Services offered on products
	Brand positions in the product line
	Additions to product line
Price	Price levels, considering consumer response, affect on sales volume, competitors
	Price changes
Promotion	Advertising: nature and content, frequency, reach of target audience, media selection
	Sales promotion
	Publicity
	Personal selling
Distribution	Nature and type of wholesale and retail outlets
	Geographical coverage
	Mark-up policy
	Trade support
	Physical distribution (transportation, storage, inventory)
	Sales force: size, territories, sales quotas, role of personal selling

Marketing plan. The plan drawn up by managers of PRODUCTS, BRANDS, or MARKETS to define objectives and action strategies. Typically a marketing plan will consist of the following sections.

1 Analysis of past marketing performance with data on the relevant market (size, growth, consumer behaviour trends), the product (sales, prices, profits), the competition (size, market share, strategies), distribution and the environment (demographic, economic, political technological trends). This leads to a statement on the company's strengths and weaknesses and the opportunities and threats facing it (see SWOT ANALYSIS).

2 Formulation of marketing objectives, related to financial objectives (profits, sales revenues, return on investment). Marketing objectives might be to increase the PRODUCT LINE'S market share by three per cent over the planning period or to increase the sales revenue of a BRAND by 5 per cent. Whenever possible, marketing objectives are stated quantitatively with a given time period for achievement.

3 Development of marketing strategies. For each objective, managers have to decide which of many strategy options to adopt. If the aim is to increase the product line's market share, a brand or brands might be selected to receive increased marketing support, or another brand might be added to the line. The brand's sales revenue might be increased by using SALES PROMOTIONS to increase the volume of sales or the price of the brand might be raised. It is at this stage of planning that the decisions are made in each of the policy areas that make up what is known as the MARKETING MIX (product, price, promotion, distribution) and co-ordinated to produce the marketing effort which will accomplish the marketing objectives.

4 Preparation of ACTION PLANS setting out what will be done, who will do it, when, and for what cost. There will be many action plans, all highly detailed.

Marketing research. The collection and analysis of information about consumers, markets and the effectiveness of marketing decisions. Modern marketing, as expressed by the MARKETING CONCEPT, would not be possible without marketing research; it is the means by which companies keep in touch with the market place. A study made in America in 1978 surveying 798 companies identified some of the many ways marketing research is used in business. Table 14 illustrates a few of those uses and indicates their importance.

Most marketing research consists of survey SAMPLING using QUESTIONNAIRES, carried out by personal interview, post, or telephone. These may be individual projects undertaken by a company's own marketing research department or by a marketing research agency. Many surveys are run by marketing research firms using panels of consumers or retail stores to keep a continuous measurement of the movement of goods (see NIELSEN).

Marketing research is not limited to consumer and industrial markets. Politicians and social scientists also benefit from it, though when used for such purposes it is called 'opinion polling' and 'social research'.

The term 'market research' is usually defined more narrowly as research into specific MARKETS, though the terms are often used interchangeably.

Table 14

Purposes of research	Per cent of companies
Measurement of market potentials	93
Determination of market characteristics	93
Market share analysis	92
Sales analysis	89
Studies of business trends	86
Competitive product studies	85
Short-range forecasting (up to one year)	85
New product acceptance and potential	84
Long-range forecasting (over one year)	82
Pricing studies	81
Testing of existing products	75
Establishment of sales quotas, territory	75

Source: Reported in Philip Kotler, *Marketing Management: Analysis, Planning and Control*, 5th edition (Prentice-Hall International, 1984).

Marketing science. Thought by critics of MARKETING to be a contradiction in terms. In so far as the methods of science are fundamental to good MARKETING RESEARCH, then of course marketing science exists. No one claims, however, that marketing is replete with 'law-like' relationships; all would agree that there is as much art as science in the implementation of marketing plans.

Nevertheless, it should be noted that there is a thriving Marketing Science Institute in Cambridge, Mass., USA, closely associated with the Harvard Business School.

Marketing Society. A professional body for senior marketing executives in the UK. The Society aims to widen understanding of marketing as a central business discipline. It holds frequent seminars and conferences, offers marketing guidance, keeps a Consultants' Register, and publishes a monthly newsletter.

Mass communications. A rather old-fashioned term for the use of the mass MEDIA for communicating with TARGET MARKETS (audiences).

Mass Observation (UK) Ltd. One of the oldest MARKETING RESEARCH agencies in the business, founded in 1937. Pioneers in social survey research.

Media. The vehicles that carry advertising – TV, radio, newspapers, magazines, posters and the mail. 'Mass media' are those that reach a national audience. (See ADVERTISING EXPENDITURE UK and ADVERTISING EXPENDITURE USA.)

Media Expenditure Analysis Ltd (MEAL). An institution in the British MARKETING RESEARCH world, for a long time compilers of statistics on advertisers' expenditures on press, TV, radio and other MEDIA.

Media planning. The decisions made by advertisers which determine the media to use for an advertising campaign and the most effective use to make of each medium, within the limits of the media budget. Planners must know how best to reach their target audience (which magazines or newspapers they read, which television programmes they watch). They must then work out the percentage of the target market they want to see the campaign (see REACH), the number of times during the campaign they want each person to have an opportunity to see the campaign (see FREQUENCY) and the cost of reaching 1000 of the target audience (see COST PER THOUSAND) for each medium. All these elements will have to be balanced out against each other to arrive finally at a media schedule which will most effectively reach the target audience.

Merchandising. 'Merchandise' refers to the goods a seller has to offer to prospective buyers. In marketing usage it has come to have some specialized meanings.

'Merchandising' can refer to efforts to increase sales of goods in retail outlets by the use of POINT OF PURCHASE DISPLAYS; in this sense, merchandisers are salespersons specializing in retail outlet productivity.

'Mass merchandising' is used to describe the kind of retailing typified by companies like Sears Roebuck (USA) and Woolworths (UK), large self-service department stores carrying a wide range of PRODUCT CLASSES and selling on a low-margin, high-turnover basis.

The term is sometimes used incorrectly (though not by marketers) to mean 'marketing'. (See SCRAMBLED MERCHANDISING.)

Me-Too. PRODUCT DIFFERENTIATION should ensure that any product introduced to the market can be distinguished from competing products. Too regularly, alas, products appear that have no differentiating qualities, other perhaps than that they are poor imitations. Such products are called 'me-too' products and face short lives and failure. Most me-too products are, by definition, not well known, but they can come from well-known companies. Aztec was meant to be Cadbury's answer to the Mars bar, but it was too like the Mars bar and had no special character of its own to attract attention. It failed as a sad me-too (see POSITIONING).

From another point of view, me-too products may be seen as indicators of the successful marketing of the copied products.

Middleman. Any member of a DISTRIBUTION CHANNEL between the manufacturer and the consumer.

Mintel. *Market Intelligence Reports*, published by Mintel Publications Ltd, are very important sources of information on consumer markets in the UK. The reports, composed from SECONDARY DATA on the basis of DESK RESEARCH, cover a wide variety of consumer markets, from adhesives to yoghurt. The company also reports on developments in retailing and on the leisure sector of the market.

Missionary selling. A technique used by a company to support the wholesaler's or distributor's sales force. A publisher's representative (the missionary salesman), for example, visits college and university teachers to inform them of the publisher's new books in their field. The teachers in turn recommend textbooks to their students who then buy the books from bookshops, and the bookshops purchase their stock from the distributor's sales representatives.

Model. A representation, either visual or verbal, of the most important elements of a complex process and their relationship with each other. The HIERARCHY OF EFFECTS, for example, is a model of the process of persuasion in advertising – from awareness, to knowledge, to liking, to preference, to conviction, to purchase. It identifies the important stages of the process and illustrates the way the process moves toward completion.

Motivation research. A form of QUALITATIVE RESEARCH, popularized by Ernest Dichter, using projective techniques (word association, sentence completion, ink-blot interpretation) to discover consumers' underlying attitudes toward products. Air-travel research led advertisers to emphasize the time-saving aspect of air travel rather than safety, since the safety appeal aroused people's fear of flying. Research into consumer attitudes to prunes revealed that the shrunken wrinkled appearance of prunes reminded people of old age. The marketing solution to the problems of prune producers was a successful new product (in the USA), bottled prune juice.

Multi-brand strategy. The practice of carrying many brands within one PRODUCT LINE, a strategy developed and practised by Procter & Gamble. It has several objectives. It is a means of obtaining greater shelf space in retail outlets, relative to competitors. It is a way of dealing with 'brand switchers', customers who like to try another brand from time to time. It is a way of dealing with would-be competitors – leaving them no gaps in the market – and of segmenting the market – providing brands which may develop their own brand-loyal followers. Finally, it is a strategy to create a degree of competition among a company's brand managers in order to keep them on their toes and at peak performance (see BRAND MANAGEMENT).

Multi-dimensional scaling. A MARKETING RESEARCH technique to measure ATTITUDES. People's attitudes, including their tastes, feelings and opinions, are complex; any attempt to define them, therefore, must use a many sided or multi-dimensional approach. Market researchers use scales to measure different degrees of attitude. Two types of scales commonly used in marketing research are the Likert Scales and the Semantic Differential Scales. In the Likert system, the respondent simply chooses the word or words which best describe his feeling towards the object being tested, and his choice is recorded on a scale of one to five. The Semantic Differential technique uses several questions about the product, each with a range of answer choices carrying negative through positive values; the number values of the respondent's answers are added to give a sum which represents the respondent's 'net' attitude toward the product. In the example shown, the summed score $(-1+0+(-2)=-3)$ indicates that the respondent dislikes yogurt. (See PERCEPTUAL MAPPING.)

Semantic Differential Scale

Do you like the taste of yogurt?

	x			
Dislike strongly (−2)	Dislike (−1)	Neutral (0)	Like (+1)	Like strongly (+2)

Is yogurt a healthful food?

		x		
Extremely not healthful (−2)	Not healthful (−1)	Neutral (0)	Healthful (+1)	Extremely healthful (+2)

Do you feel your friends like yogurt?

x				
Dislike strongly (−2)	Dislike (−1)	Neutral (0)	Like (+1)	Like strongly (+2)

(For Likert Scale see p. 94.)

Likert Scale

Do you like yogurt?

Dislike extremely (=1)	Dislike (=2)	Neutral (=3)	Like (=4)	Like extremely (=5)

Multiples. A multiple is a company that has shops in many high streets or shopping centres. In the UK, multiples now dominate the grocery, clothing and electrical goods businesses, as Sainsbury's, Next and Dixon's attest. (See RETAILERS.)

N

National account management. The large national retail chains buy in very large quantities and consequently negotiate trading terms from a position of considerable power. A company hoping to sell to Tesco (UK) or J. C. Penney (USA) will have to consider very carefully how to pitch for their business. Many manufacturers now have special marketing teams, national account teams, to deal with the 'trade', as it is called in the UK. Because they negotiate prices (and very large sums of money will be at stake in terms of profit margins), a senior marketing executive will usually lead the national account team. Negotiations with large grocery chains involve not only price but also the amount of shelf space (facings) that will be given to products. National account management today tests the marketing skill of even the largest manufacturers.

National Advertising Review Board. The advertising industry's watchdog body in the USA. It uses moral persuasion against agencies which break the industry's own codes of practice. (See FEDERAL TRADE COMMISSION.)

National brand. See MANUFACTURER BRAND.

National Consumer Council (NCC). Set up in 1975 by the UK government, its main aim is to safeguard the interests of consumers and to represent the voice of the consumer to government and industry. It deals only with issues of policy.

National launch. The method of introducing a new product into the market by making it available throughout the entire market at one time rather than by distributing it gradually, area by area. (See ROLLING LAUNCH.)

National Readership Survey. See JOINT INDUSTRY COMMITTEE FOR NATIONAL READERSHIP SURVEYS.

New product development (NPD). The range of activities involved in conceiving, developing, and launching new products into the market. It is a critically important process since most

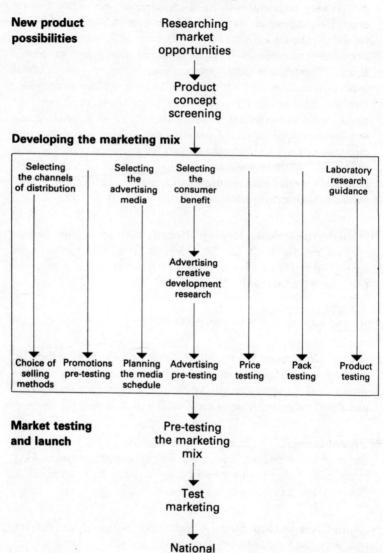

New product development

New product possibilities

Researching market opportunities

↓

Product concept screening

Developing the marketing mix

| Selecting the channels of distribution | | Selecting the advertising media | Selecting the consumer benefit | | | Laboratory research guidance |

Advertising creative development research

| Choice of selling methods | Promotions pre-testing | Planning the media schedule | Advertising pre-testing | Price testing | Pack testing | Product testing |

Market testing and launch

Pre-testing the marketing mix

↓

Test marketing

↓

National market monitoring

(*Source:* John Downham, *Market Research,* reproduced with permission from Unilever Educational Liaison.)

firms have to introduce new products into their PRODUCT LINE frequently in order to retain a COMPETITIVE ADVANTAGE. Failure rates are high. Only about half the new products placed on the market become commercially viable, and only one in 40 new product ideas ever becomes a successful product. (See INNOVATION.)

Nielsen. The A. C. Nielsen Co. was founded in 1939 in the USA. It offers a wide range of MARKETING RESEARCH services in the USA and the UK including the well-known shop auditing service, the Nielsen Index. Continuous measurements are made of sales from retail food outlets, drug stores/chemists, liquor stores and CASH AND CARRY wholesalers.

The Nielsen Food Index in the UK, for example, covers 857 grocers, selected to allow analysis of patterns of trading by shop type (grocers, co-operatives, multiples, independents) in nine regional areas. Audits are conducted bi-monthly. Clients subscribe to the Index, and according to their requirements, reports can be made for brands, brand size, flavour, etc. Reports cover details on consumer sales, retailer purchases, sources of delivery, retailer stocks, stock cover, prices, distribution and advertising expenditure.

In the USA, Nielsen also sells audience research data.

Non-durable goods. Goods such as grocery products which are consumed rapidly and frequently and are therefore made widely and conveniently available.

Non-probability sampling. SAMPLING techniques in MARKETING RESEARCH in which the researcher uses personal discretion instead of random selection in identifying the sample, thereby reducing the statistical validity of the results. Where statistical precision is not the first priority, non-probability sampling can give useful results – and is usually cheaper. The two methods widely used by marketers are QUOTA SAMPLING and JUDGEMENT SAMPLING.

Non-profit marketing. The application of the MARKETING CONCEPT to organizations that operate in the non-profit sector. Symphony orchestras, art galleries, universities and the armed services are strictly speaking not in the business of seeking out profits although they are in an EXCHANGE relationship with their public. Many such organizations have applied the marketing concept to their activities, such as art museums (retail shops) and the armed services (advertising campaigns).

O

Odd-even pricing. A pricing convention used in retailing whereby a product is priced with a figure ending in five or nine which is not far below a whole number. Thus 99p will be used in preference to £1, or $24.95 in preference to $25.00. Whether consumers actually think or even feel that 'odd' priced goods are better value than 'even' priced goods has not been proven.

Off-the-peg research. MARKETING RESEARCH that uses data that have been collected by someone other than the researcher. The four main types of material for off-the-peg research are published sources (see SECONDARY DATA), data regularly collected and sold by marketing research companies (see SYNDICATED RESEARCH), data on specialist subjects regularly collected and sold by marketing research companies (see SPECIALIST RESEARCH), and data commissioned from syndicated surveys (see OMNIBUS RESEARCH).

Office of Fair Trading (OFT). Established by the Fair Trading Act in 1973 in the UK to encourage fair competition, its main task is to review all trade practices which may adversely affect consumers. It has four divisions: consumer affairs (codes of practice enforcement, mail-order protection), credit (administration of the Consumer Credit Act 1974), monopolies and mergers, and restrictive practices.

Omnibus research. Omnibus surveys are based on questionnaires that are sent out regularly to a panel of respondents by MARKETING RESEARCH companies. Space on the questionnaire is available to firms who have specific market research needs. Because anyone can buy a place on the questionnaire, it is called an omnibus survey. Omnibus research is an efficient and relatively cheap way of obtaining PRIMARY DATA. The MARKET RESEARCH SOCIETY's *Yearbook* lists firms providing survey facilities. (See OFF–THE–PEG RESEARCH.)

Open-ended question. A question used in MARKETING RESEARCH which requires an answer other than 'yes', 'no' or 'don't know'. Examples might be 'What features do you look for in considering the purchase of a new car?' or 'What factors do you think are important in preparing meals for your family?' The respondent is free to answer in whatever way he wants. Open-ended questions are used in semi-structured interviews (see STRUCTURED INTERVIEW) and in GROUP DISCUSSION, where attitudes and opinions are of concern to the researcher.

Opinion leaders. Persons who influence the purchasing behaviour of others, often by word of mouth or example (See REFERENCE GROUPS). Opinion leaders are not necessarily the first to adopt a new product or idea (see INNOVATORS), but their acceptance of it is vitally important to its ultimate success. If they can be reached by MEDIA advertising, then the multiplier effect will come into play to greatly widen public acceptance of the product. (See DIFFUSION OF INNOVATION.)

Opinion polls. Consumer research concerned specifically with politics. Opinion polling is now a central element in political campaigns on both sides of the Atlantic. Public opinion polls are commissioned by the MEDIA (mainly newspapers and television) for public consumption. Private opinion polling is commissioned by the political parties and their candidates to help them develop campaign strategy.

Sample sizes vary. *Time* magazine published polls during the last USA presidential election campaign, conducted by Yankelovich, Skelly and White, based upon telephone calls to 1000 voters nationwide. MORI's polls for the London *Evening Standard* are based on face-to-face interviews with nearly 2000 electors at 173 sampling points throughout the country.

Some MARKETING RESEARCH agencies have become famous for their opinion polling: Gallup (USA and UK), Harris (USA and UK), Marplan (UK), NOP (National Opinion Polls, UK), MORI (UK), Elmo Roper (USA). In the USA, the American Association for Public Opinion Research and in Europe, the European Society for Opinion and Marketing Research (ESOMAR) are both professional associations representing agencies working in the field of opinion polling.

Opportunities to see (OTS). See FREQUENCY.

Optical character recognition (OCR). An electronic optical scanner which reads pre-coded information from QUESTIONNAIRES directly into a computer for data processing, greatly speeding up the collation and analysis of data, with obvious application to MARKETING RESEARCH.

Organizational buying. The way in which organizations, as contrasted with individuals, identify, evaluate and choose the products they buy. An automobile manufacturer, for example, buys hundreds of components from accessory suppliers. The company's negotiations with such suppliers may start at the early stages of research and development of a new model and continue right through until that model is replaced. The nature of the relationship will evolve over this period, from designing new components to maintaining supplies in dealer service outlets. (See BUYGRID and BUYING CENTRE.)

Own label. See DEALER BRAND.

P

Packaging. In most retailing today, products come in packages; indeed, the package has become an integral part of the PRODUCT. It protects the product, promotes and advertises the product (labelling design, coupons, reusable containers) and may display the product or make it more visible. It may be a convenient means for dispensing contents (liquid soaps, oil, glue, toothpaste), and may carry important information about the contents of the product (required by law) and directions for its use.

Paired comparisons. A technique used in MARKETING RESEARCH which asks consumers to rank their product preferences. They are presented with a pair of products or brands and asked to choose the one they prefer. Soft drink research might use the following pairs:

Coke – Pepsi	Pepsi – 7-Up
Coke – 7-Up	Pepsi – Dr Pepper
Coke – Dr Pepper	Pepsi – Fresca
Dr Pepper – Fresca	7-Up – Dr Pepper
7-Up – Fresca	Coke – Fresca

The results will show the number of times each brand was preferred in comparison with another. Fresca, for example, might be preferred in every pairing and receive a rating of four, Pepsi might be preferred three times, and so on. The final figures will reveal an order of brand preference.

Pareto principle. The Pareto principle is sometimes referred to as the 80–20 rule, and though hardly a scientific principle, it appears to be present in many marketing relationships. For example, many companies seem to derive 80 per cent of their profits from 20 per cent of their PRODUCT LINE. Some companies sell 80 per cent of their output through 20 per cent of their distributive outlets. In other words, the Pareto principle invites marketing companies to analyse the PRODUCTIVITY of their marketing effort to discover whether the kind of imbalance illustrated by the Pareto principle exists – and if so, to do something about it!

Penetration strategy. The use of low prices and heavy advertising to increase MARKET SHARE. When a company has a product in a market supplied by products that are relatively similar to one another, it may decide to use penetration strategy to increase its product's market share. For penetration strategy to be attempted, the market will have to be large enough for the company to be able to sustain relatively low profit margins. The strategy has the added advantage that it may deter potential new entrants into the market because profit possibilities may appear limited.

Perception. The process by which an individual receives, selects and interprets information. Marketers, and advertising specialists in particular, are very interested in the phenomenon of perception and try to find the signals that will produce in the consumer a favourable view or perception of their product (the product's IMAGE). When the signals are right, advertising can be very powerful; people's perceptions of products often owe more to skillful advertising than to any intrinsic or exclusive qualities the products may possess. Thus, Ivory is the 'pure' soap, Charmin (USA) is the 'soft' toilet tissue and Guinness the beer that is good for you. (See POSITIONING.)

Perceptual mapping. A technique borrowed from mathematical psychology and used by marketers to understand the structure of a MARKET. Consumers develop an IMAGE of a product based on its particular features or its benefits (real or imagined) or its price. These perceptions can be identified (see QUALITATIVE RESEARCH) and products then plotted on a graph or map (see example on p. 104). The closer two brands are on the map, the closer they are in competition. If research has also identified the characteristics of an 'ideal' product, then the closer a brand is to that point, the more likely it is to be preferred over the others. Gaps on the map may represent potential market opportunities. (see MULTI-DIMENSIONAL SCALING and POSITIONING).

Personal selling. Direct, face-to-face communication between buyer and seller. Personal selling is as old as marketing itself (see DIRECT MARKETING). In industrial goods' marketing, personal selling is generally more important than ADVERTISING, because the salesman often has to meet the particular, perhaps unique, requirements of each customer.

Physical distribution. The actual movement of goods from the

A Perceptual Map

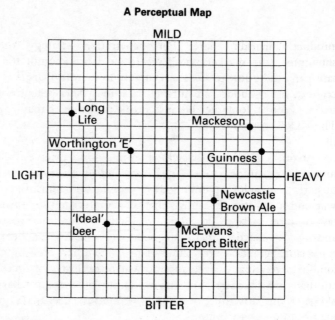

(*Source:* S. Crouch, *Marketing Research for Managers*, Pan Books, 1985)

point of production to the point of consumption, usually involving ordering, transportation, warehousing and storage, and inventory control. (See DISTRIBUTION.)

Piloting. The testing of a QUESTIONNAIRE before it is used in a MARKETING RESEARCH survey. The questionnaire is a vital and frequently used research instrument, and its construction requires great skill if it is to yield the sort of information sought by the researcher. It is usual, therefore, to try it out before its release for field work. Interviewers conduct an interview in a normal way and note any difficulties that arise. The feedback from this trial run is then used to redesign those parts of the questionnaire that cause problems.

Planned shopping centres. Planned shopping centres are a relatively new development in retailing and are still variable in form. They are clusters of businesses, primarily retailers (often including one dominant department store), located either in a single structure or in a related set of buildings and usually controlled by a management belonging to the centre developer. They are now found all over the world and are beginning to create their own cultures, quite different from high street or neighbourhood shopping centres. The newer ones in the USA contain restaurants, FAST FOOD franchises and movie houses. They may be covered with elaborate glass structures and environmentally controlled, having fountains and pools, skating rinks and gardens. They are large enough to provide a full day's entertainment for the family.

Planning. A basic function of management that involves setting objectives, developing strategies to achieve the objectives and working out tactics to implement the strategies. Some manifestation of the process will be found at every level of management and may be called by various names. When it is carried out by top management, it is called corporate planning and involves long-term company objectives, broad directions in which the company should move, and allocation of resources (see CORPORATE PLAN). At lower levels it becomes marketing planning and may be applied to PRODUCT LINES or groups of product lines, single products or BRANDS, or MARKETS (see MARKETING PLAN).

When planning focusses on developing broad strategies for action over time, it is called strategic planning. (Since corporate plans are concerned only with broad strategies, they are sometimes called strategic plans instead of corporate plans.) Strategic planning has become very important over the last decade or so, reflecting the switch in managerial interest from short-term profits with hope for tomorrow to planned long-term profitability. In large complex companies, strategic planning provides a framework in which the strategies developed at one level of management become the objectives of managers at lower levels.

Regardless of the level at which planning occurs, the first step is one of situation analysis and evaluation. Many sophisticated analytical tools are available to managers: PORTFOLIO ANALYSIS to show the profitability potential of products: SWOT ANALYSIS and ENVIRONMENTAL SCANNING techniques to indicate internal strengths and weaknesses and point out marketing opportunities or dangers.

At each planning level, the same pattern of analysis and evaluation and formulation of objectives and strategy takes place until at the end of the chain the many detailed ACTION PLANS on which the corporate plan depends are drawn up and executed.

It should be said that the planning process, though of critical importance to a company's success, is easier to describe than do, and companies vary widely in the degree to which they apply and succeed in effective marketing planning.

Point of purchase display. In most retail outlets, opportunities exist to mount special displays of certain products. The term, point of purchase display, refers to special displays such as counter-top cardboard constructions (frequently used to sell cosmetics) or more elaborate freestanding creations (common in supermarkets). (See MERCHANDISING and SALES PROMOTION.)

Point of sale. Where the culmination of the whole marketing effort – the sale – takes place. The term usually refers to a retail store, but with the advent of self service and the technology revolution, it may now also mean the checkout counter (see ELECTRONIC POINT OF SALE).

Portfolio analysis. Borrowed from investment portfolio analysis and used by MARKETING MANAGEMENT to evaluate a company's product offerings for the purpose of determining how best to allocate company resources. There are several different methods of product portfolio analysis in current use, such as the Boston Consulting Group's GROWTH/SHARE MATRIX, GENERAL ELECTRIC BUSINESS SCREEN, and Shell International's DIRECTIONAL POLICY MATRIX, but they all involve an analysis of the profitability, prospects and investment requirements of the company's products.

A company's ideal PRODUCT MIX consists of a balance between products which are very profitable and those which are expected to become very profitable, the cash flowing in from the former being available for investment in support of the latter. Product portfolio analysis enables marketing managers to decide which of their products to channel resources into or away from, which products to consider for deletion, and where opportunities to add new products exist, in order that the desired balance of products might be attained.

Product portfolio analysis is a tool of strategic PLANNING that can be used at more than one level of management. In a large multi-product company, it is applied at top management level to the company's STRATEGIC BUSINESS UNITS (SBUs), separate divisions each handling one of the company's PRODUCT LINES. It may also be used by SBU and other managers to analyse the products under their responsibility. (See HARVESTING STRATEGY, PRODUCT ELIMINATION, MARKETING PLAN and PLANNING.)

Positioning. The attempt by marketers to give a product a certain identity or IMAGE, so that consumers will perceive the product as having distinctive features or benefits relative to competing products.

Positioning may be looked at from the point of view of the consumer or from the point of view of the marketer, and it may be better understood if it is illustrated.

Suppose a shopper goes to the supermarket to buy a brand of washing-up liquid/dishwashing detergent and wants one that is gentle to hands. Chances are that the choice will be Fairy Liquid (UK) or Ivory Liquid (USA). These are the brands that are in firm hold of the 'gentle to hands' position in the washing-up detergent market, from the shopper's point of view. If the shopper had wanted, instead, just a good functional detergent at a reasonable price, the choice would probably have been the supermarket's own brand. DEALER BRANDS hold the 'reliable and cheap(er)' position in the market. But suppose there is another brand of washing-up liquid on the shelf, called Wash-up. It is gentle to hands (the label says so) and it is competitive in price. But it doesn't sell because the brand name doesn't mean those things to the consumer.

If the marketers of Wash-up don't want to see the product fail, they must decide how to make the brand mean something to the consumer. They must position Wash-up. Two choices are open to them. Because they know Wash-up is chemically gentle to hands, they can decide to try to implant the name Wash-up in the minds of consumers as a 'gentle to hands' detergent – alongside the name of Fairy Liquid and in direct competition with it. The chances of success for this strategy are slim. Once a consumer has associated a brand name with a position, the bonding tends to last, to the effective exclusion of all others. With massive effort, Pepsi Cola have managed to take a share of the cola market from Coca Cola, but not to become the market leader nor to oust Coke as the name that means cola. Avis decided to compete in a position already strongly held by Hertz and succeeded, not by toppling the leader, but by associating the name Avis with the leader – 'We're Number Two. We try harder'. But Hertz remains the market leader in the car-hire business.

The second choice open to Wash-up's marketers is to try to find a 'position' in the washing-up liquid market that no other brand owns. They might discover, for example, that changing lifestyles had created an unfilled 'masculine' position. If they decide it is a good idea to position Wash-up as the washing-up liquid for the man of the house, they would proceed to use all the elements of the MARKETING MIX – packaging, promotion, and especially advertising ('strong and gentle', perhaps) – to produce a brand that consumers would recognize and accept as 'the washing-up liquid for men'.

Product positioning is well illustrated in the very large shampoo market, where there are brands for 'beautiful hair', 'healthy hair', 'blow-dried hair', 'frequently washed hair', 'hair over forty', 'dandruff control', etc.

Posters. An advertising medium accounting for less than ten per cent of advertising expenditure but forming a striking part of the landscape of most cities. In the UK there are about 200,000 poster sites, the largest of which are freestanding and are called supersites. Supersite advertisements, are often painted, whereas smaller posters are usually pasted onto buildings. Popularly called billboards in the USA and hoardings in the UK.

Premium offers. A form of SALES PROMOTION which offers a customer the opportunity of obtaining one product, often at an attractive price, by purchasing another (very popular with cosmetic and toiletry manufacturers). It is a device to promote the sale of the product on the shelf.

Pre-testing. A MARKETING RESEARCH technique to predict the effectiveness of an advertisement before it is released. An ADVERTISING AGENCY will define the objectives of a piece of MEDIA advertising and then test it, using GROUP DISCUSSION, to determine the extent to which the objectives will be realized. Print advertising is sometimes tested by split runs, in which different advertisements are alternated and readers' responses to each are measured. The Schwerin test is well known in the USA as a device for testing

TV and radio commercials. Before being exposed to the commercial being tested, respondents are asked to choose a brand. After seeing the advertisement, they are asked to choose again, and any change in their selection is considered a measure of the effectiveness of the commercial.

Price discrimination. When intermediaries or industrial buyers purchase products of similar quality and in similar quantity, they expect to buy on the same terms. If the seller favours one or more of his customers, and the difference in price cannot be justified on cost terms, an offence has been committed under the Clayton and Robinson–Patman Acts (USA).

In the UK, if products are sold to different classes of customers (PRODUCT MARKETS), price discrimination appears to be allowed. For example, a builder purchasing from a builders' supply company will usually obtain lower prices than an individual home owner buying the same materials from the same supplier. The favourable 'trade prices' appear to be discriminating against individual consumers, but since the two types of customers represent different product markets, the price discrimination is allowed.

Price elasticity. The relationship between the price of a product and the quantity of that product bought by consumers (quantity demanded). It is expressed by marketers as the percentage change in quantity demanded resulting from each percentage change in price. When the percentage change in quantity demanded is less than the percentage change in price, then price is said to be inelastic and when the percentage change in quantity demanded is more than the percentage change in price, demand is said to be elastic.

The demand for some products is very sensitive to price. The number of package tours sold, for example, fluctuates as prices rise or fall. Other products are relatively insensitive to price: increases in the price of petrol/gasoline do not result in significant decreases in consumption.

In determining pricing policy, marketers need to be able to predict the effect price changes will have on demand for their products. If price is elastic, changes in consumer demand for a product reflect changes in the product's price; if price is inelastic, demand is relatively insensitive to changes in price.

Primary data. Data collected at source for specific research purposes, using carefully designed data-collection tools such as QUESTIONNAIRES or interviews. (See SECONDARY DATA.)

Private label. See DEALER BRAND.

Problem children. Brands with low market shares in high growth markets whose future profitability is uncertain. High investment in them by their companies involves high risk. It might – or might not – pay off. (See GROWTH/SHARE MATRIX.)

Product. A simple word but in marketing terms it is a complicated concept. A product is anything that can be offered to the MARKET that might satisfy a need or want. It may be an object, a service, a place, an organization or an idea.

Products can be thought about at three levels. Every product has a core benefit or service, known as the 'core product'. We rarely think about products only in terms of core benefit, however. Products have BRAND names, PACKAGING, qualities and styling, for example – these make up the 'tangible product'. Beyond the tangible product is the 'augmented product', which includes WARRANTIES, guarantees, after-sales service, installation, delivery, credit. The augmented product is usually perceived by the consumer to be the product he buys.

Product class. A term applied to the largest grouping of products that have similar functions. Cigarettes, automobiles and microcomputers are each a product class. Also called 'product category'.

Product differentiation. The practice of making one product distinguishable from all other products. In virtually every PRODUCT CLASS there are many products performing similar functions and needing to be differentiated from each other. Not only must one company's brands be distinguishable from competing brands, but frequently from each other. Products may be differentiated by quality, features, styling, price, service. They may be differentiated by ADVERTISING and SALES PROMOTION, by which the marketer trying to develop special consumer ATTITUDES towards a brand. Type of retail outlet may also differentiate products.

"We have high quality and low prices. Which do you want?"

If consumers can distinguish between products in a MARKET and if they can state a preference for one BRAND over another, then product differentiation has succeeded. If product differentiation fails, ME-TOO products are the result.

Product elimination. The orderly process for withdrawing a product from the market (also called product deletion). Products do not normally live forever. For most, profitable life is short; even long-lived products can eventually go into decline. Many companies do not like to face this fact and through poor management

111

or nostalgia keep products in the family of product offerings even though they may be losing money for the company. Good management requires regular monitoring of a company's PRO-DUCT MIX to assess each product's profitability status (see PORT-FOLIO ANALYSIS).

An unprofitable product is not always an overall liability to a company, however. In some cases it may contribute to the ease of selling other products. Car dealers, for example, may consider their reputations for excellent service are enhanced by stocking accessories for non-current models, products that in themselves are unprofitable to the manufacturer.

Products which have been marked for deletion, if they have been familiar brands, may be 'harvested', made to produce a short-term profit before they are finally withdrawn (see HARVESTING STRATEGY).

Product life cycle. A concept that has attracted marketers for many years. Using the biological analogy, it is argued that all products are born, introduced to the market, grow in sales, mature (sales growth stops) and then decline (sales fall). This cycle is described by the sales curve and by the profit curve in the following diagram.

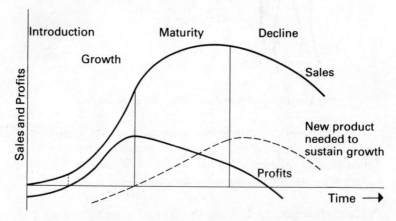

It is tempting to deduce from this life cycle that it will there-fore be possible to predict movements in the sales curve, hence to develop marketing strategies appropriate to each stage in the life cycle (see p. 113).

Implications of the product life cycle

	Introduction	Growth	Maturity	Decline
CHARACTERISTICS				
SALES	Low	Fast growth	Slow growth	Decline
PROFITS	Negligible	Peak levels	Declining	Low or zero
CASH FLOW	Negative	Moderate	High	Low
CUSTOMERS	Innovative	Mass market	Mass market	Laggards
COMPETITORS	Few	Growing	Many rivals	Declining number
RESPONSES				
STRATEGIC FOCUS	Expand market	Market penetration	Defend share	Productivity
MKG. EXPENDITURES	High	High (declining %)	Falling	Low
MKG. EMPHASIS	Product awareness	Brand preference	Brand loyalty	Selective
DISTRIBUTION	Patchy	Intensive	Intensive	Selective
PRICE	High	Lower	Lowest	Rising
PRODUCT	Basic	Improved	Differentiated	Rationalised

(*Source*: P. Doyle, 'The realities of the product life cycle', *Quarterly Review of Marketing*, **1**(4), Summer 1976)

Critics of the concept of the life cycle point out that the shape of the sales curve, far from being pre-ordained, is a function of the marketing effort put behind the product; hence the life cycle has no value as a forecasting tool. Furthermore, critics point to brands which appear to demonstrate no life cycle. Many have been mature for years and show no signs of decline, as for example those listed in Table 15. The table shows brands that were leaders in their respective product classes in 1923 (for the USA) and in 1933 (for the UK) and whose current positions (1984) are still No. 1.

Product line. A group of closely related products marketed by a company. Companies may have one or many product lines, and product lines may contain few or many products. Heinz has one product line consisting of many different food items, while Procter & Gamble has many product lines – detergents, disposable diapers/nappies, toothpaste, etc. The number of products within a product line is related to the number of consumer segments a company can identify and supply. (See MULTI-BRAND STRATEGY.)

Product management. See BRAND MANAGEMENT.

Product management hierarchy. There are three levels of product management. The bottom level is BRAND MANAGEMENT; each of the company's brands has a different manager. The next level in PRODUCT LINE management, headed by product line or product group managers. At the top level is PRODUCT MIX management, headed by the marketing director or marketing vice-president but actually the responsibility of all top management.

Product market. A company's PRODUCT LINE is frequently sold to several different classes of customer, each having distinct requirements. A line of food products, for example, may be sold to the retail market (grocery outlets), to the catering market (restaurants and hotels) and to the institutional market (schools, hospitals, military installations, prisons). Each product market requires a different marketing approach.

Product mix. All the products offered to consumers by a com-

Table 15 *The long life of strong brands*

US brand leader		UK brand leader	
Year: 1923	Current position	Year: 1933	Current position
Campbell's, soup	No.1	Brooke Bond, tea	No.1
Coca-Cola, soft drinks	No.1	Cadbury's, chocolate	No.1
Ever Ready, batteries	No.1	Colgate, toothpaste	No.1
Gillette, razors	No.1	Ever Ready, batteries	No.1
Gold Medal, flour	No.1	Gillette, razors	No.1
Ivory, soap	No.1	Hoover, vacuum cleaners	No.1
Kodak, cameras	No.1	Johnson's, floor polish	No.1
Life Savers, mint candies	No.1	Kellogg's, cornflakes	No.1
Nabisco, biscuits	No.1	Kodak, film	No.1
Sherwin-Williams, paint	No.1	Rowntree's, pastilles	No.1
Singer, sewing machines	No.1	Schweppes, mixers	No.1
Wrigley, chewing gum	No.1	Stork, margarine	No.1

Source: extracts from Saatchi and Saatchi Co. Plc, *Annual Report 1984.*

pany. The product mix is described in terms of its width, length, depth and consistency. Width is the number of different PRODUCT LINES a company offers (Procter & Gamble sell detergents, soaps, toothpaste, deodorants, disposable diapers/nappies and, in the USA, coffee). Length refers to the number of BRANDS of each product (P&G have seven brands of soap). Depth is determined by the number of variants each brand may have (soap may come in hand size, bath size, guest size, family size, etc.). Consistency defines the extent to which the product lines are related. Procter & Gamble's product lines are consistent in so far as all the items are grocery products and sell through grocery outlets.

Product orientation. Describes the view that management used to take – and sometimes still does – that products come first, and persuading consumers to buy them, second. It is a view now largely superseded by MARKET ORIENTATION, by which companies first find out what products customers want and then try to produce them profitably. Put another way, the product-oriented company says 'We will sell what we produce', while the market-oriented company says 'We will produce only what we know we can sell' (see diagram on p. 116).

Product testing. In the early stages of NEW PRODUCT DEVELOP-

Product orientation

| Products | → | Selling and promotion | → | Profits through sales volume |

Market orientation

| Customers | → | Integrated marketing | → | Profits through customer satisfaction |

MENT, prototypes or even product concepts may be tested, using groups of potential users (see CONCEPT TESTING and HALL TESTS). In the final stage before market launch, products may be the subjects of MARKET TESTS.

Productivity. The relationship between marketing output (sales) and marketing inputs (expenditures). Productivity in marketing is a neglected subject. Marketing uses resources, and it is therefore important to examine the relationship between sales and the inputs that go into the marketing effort.

If inputs can be used more efficiently, greater profitability will result. If the effects of ADVERTISING on sales can be understood, it should be possible to predict the effect an increase in advertising expenditures will have on sales. If the increase in sales is greater than the cost of the increased advertising, profits will increase and productivity will have been improved. This approach explains why productivity measurement is often referred to in marketing as profitability control. (See MARKETING AUDIT.)

Profit centre. An organizational unit within a company, responsible for showing a profit. Marketing managers, for example, may be responsible for the profit performance of the company's PRODUCT MIX, a PRODUCT LINE, or even a single product. Any function in an organization under the control of a manager charged with producing a profit from that operation is known as a profit centre. (See STRATEGIC BUSINESS UNIT.)

Profit Impact of Market Strategy (PIMS). Arising out of studies undertaken at General Electric (USA) in the 1960s, an extensive research project was set up first at the Marketing Science Institute and subsequently at the Strategic Planning Institute (both located in Cambridge, Massachusetts). PIMS has developed an extensive data base in the USA (a similar data base is growing in the UK) that throws light on the major factors that explain variability of return on investment (ROI) in a wide variety of industries. In 1983 the PIMS data base in the USA had 250 companies, controlling 3000 separate businesses. PIMS data have provided researchers and business mnagers with many insights into what determines profitability in the market place.

Psychographics. A basis for segmenting consumer markets based on SOCIAL CLASS, LIFESTYLE and personality. Social class influences consumer preferences for food, clothing, home furnishings, leisure activities, retailers. Lifestyle is very often expressed by the kinds of products people buy: sporty, conservative, large or small cars, convenience foods or wholefoods. Personality is reflected in people's choice of cars, cosmetics and drinks.

Public relations (PR). As defined by the INSTITUTE OF PUBLIC RELATIONS, 'the means by which an organization tries to develop a mutual understanding between itself and its public'. While much PR work is concerned with handling press conferences and press releases, PR covers a much wider range of activities. A company's relations with government, with consumer groups, with trade unions, for instance, may all appropriately involve public relations, where the development of mutual understanding is important. In fact, it is often argued that PR is a two-way means of communication, as much about listening as about telling.

Public relations should be an integral part of the communications component of the MARKETING MIX, since it can increase marketing effectiveness.

Punter. British marketing slang for the consumer. The word more commonly describes gamblers – those who put bets on horses or buy shares in the stock market. Perhaps the term is quite properly applied to those who risk their money in the market place.

Push money. Money given to retailers by manufacturers or wholesalers to be used to reward salespersons who aggressively sell certain items, perhaps new products, slow-moving items or high-priced items. Push money is also known as 'SPIFFS' in the USA.

Push *vs* pull strategies. Two different ways to move CONSUMER PRODUCTS through a DISTRIBUTION CHANNEL. Most companies have to utilize a push strategy to move their goods through a distribution channel. If their goods are to reach the consumer, they must persuade each member of the distribution channel to stock their products, using trade discounts, PERSONAL SELLING, ADVERTISING ALLOWANCES, etc. Large and rich companies, on the other hand, may utilize a pull strategy. By investing large sums of money in ADVERTISING and SALES PROMOTION they can create consumer demand for their products, and consumer demand at the end of the distribution channel is a powerful reason (pull) for channel members to handle a company's goods.

Q

Qualitative research. MARKETING RESEARCH designed to gain insights into consumers' attitudes, perceptions and motivations. Unlike QUANTITATIVE RESEARCH, it does not attempt to produce results that are statistically measurable. Its methods are chiefly GROUP DISCUSSION and DEPTH INTERVIEW, and the number of respondents involved in a research session is small, perhaps 50 or fewer.

Qualitative research is widely used in the process of NEW PRODUCT DEVELOPMENT to elicit consumer views of desirable and undesirable product features. Advertising copy is normally tested before release, when agencies sometimes discover that consumers receive messages rather different from the ones intended. It is also frequently used in the early stages of the development of a research project to give researchers a 'feel' for the situation. Some qualitative research studies may be followed up by large-scale quantitative research surveys.

Quantitative research. MARKETING RESEARCH using SAMPLING techniques which permit results to be expressed quantitatively within acceptable margins of error. Its methods allow collected data to be measured with reasonable accuracy. It is the kind of research that can reveal what proportion of the population owns video recorders, or watches 'Dallas', or drinks beer. It is distinguished from QUALITATIVE RESEARCH which is concerned with attitudes and motivations.

Quantity discount. A price reduction given to a customer who buys in quantity; the larger the quantity purchased, the larger the discount. Quantity discounts are usually offered by manufacturers to wholesalers, but may also be offered by wholesalers to retailers. Retail grocery chains, because they buy in large quantities, negotiate quantity discounts directly with manufacturers.

Questionnaire. The primary tool of MARKETING RESEARCH, used in survey SAMPLING. It is a device for delivering questions to respondents and recording their answers. A questionnaire has four main purposes: to collect relevant data, to make data comparable, to minimize bias in the asking of questions and recording of responses and to frame questions in a varied and interesting way so that respondents will answer without resentment.

The design of the questionnaire is of great importance to the success of the research. It must cover all the information that is needed to meet the objectives of the research. The questions must be easy to understand and unambiguous and the question-naire must not be too long. (See STRUCTURED INTERVIEW.)

Quota sampling. The selection of respondents in a sample so as to represent age, sex, class, region, etc., in the same proportion as that which exists for the population as a whole. Widely used in MARKETING RESEARCH. A quota sheet as used by an interviewer is shown opposite. (See NON-PROBABILITY SAMPLING.)

Your assignment is to interview 30 respondents to the sex, age and class quotas detailed below.

Sex

	Required	Achieved	Total
Male	15		
Female	15		
			30

Age

	Required	Achieved	Total
16–34	13		
35–54	12		
55+	5		
			30

Class

	Required	Achieved	Total
ABC1	12		
C2	11		
DE	7		
			30

(*Source:* S. Crouch, *Marketing Research for Managers*, Pan Books, 1985)

R

Rack jobbers. An American term for a form of very limited service wholesaling. Rack jobbers specialize in providing grocery stores and supermarkets with non-food items which are usually sold from racks provided by the rack jobbers themselves. Typical items will be health and beauty aids, houseware and hardware goods, books, records and tapes. The rack jobber is paid in cash for the stock sold or delivered.

There is no equivalent in the UK. Grocery retailers who handle non-grocery items usually stock them themselves and are not serviced by an independent MIDDLEMAN.

Random sampling. See SAMPLING.

Rate card. A list of advertising prices charged by a member of the MEDIA. A TV rate card might show the cost of a 30-second spot at different times of the day. Rate cards are used by ADVERTISING AGENCIES in planning their use of the media, but they are also of interest to marketing managers (particularly brand managers) who have advertising budgets to prepare.

Reach. The proportion of a total target market that an advertiser wants to reach at least once in an advertising campaign over a given period of time. If the target market is made up of about one million people and the objective is to reach 80 per cent of them, 800,000 people will have to be exposed to the advertising over the given period. (See MEDIA PLANNING.)

Recall tests. MARKETING RESEARCH tests for measuring how much consumers remember about advertisements, used in both PRE-TESTING and post-testing advertising. Unaided recall tests reveal which advertisements respondents can spontaneously remember. Aided recall tests show which advertisements they can remember from a series they have seen in an advertising campaign. Recognition tests are used to measure campaign penetration: respondents look through newspapers or magazines they have already read to see which advertisements they remember.

Reciprocity. Simply stated, reciprocity means 'If you buy from me, I'll buy from you'. Reciprocity operates in industrial markets, where buyers and sellers have close relationships. Reciprocal trade can operate on a friendly basis where both parties see some advantage in such an arrangement and enter into it voluntarily.

The legality of reciprocity has never been seriously challenged, as long as the practice benefits both parties. If it involves coercion or conspiracy, it is illegal.

Reference groups. Social groups on which consumers model their behaviour. A reference group may be friends, neighbours or colleagues, or it may be a group one admires or aspires to belong to, such as 'yuppies' (young and upwardly mobile professionals) or 'punk rockers'. Reference-group influence is strongest where highly conspicuous products are concerned, such as clothes, cars, drinks and high-tech equipment.

Marketers recognize the power of this influence and expend much effort in associating a product with the appropriate reference group.

Relaunch. The reintroduction of an existing brand into the market after changes have been made to it (see REPOSITIONING). A good example is Colgate's recent relaunch of Palmolive soap, at a cost of £7 million. The brand is now targeted more specifically at the health-conscious user. It has undergone 'cosmetic' changes (a new softer shade of the original green, a more rounded shape and new packaging). It is supported by a £2.5 million television campaign, emphasizing the skin-care attributes of the product, and by heavy sales promotions – free samples with Colgate Toothpaste, all three sizes of the soap at trial prices, FLASH PACKS of the bath size.

Nabisco has also relaunched Shredded Wheat, based not on a change in the product but on new publicity about the dietary qualities of the old product, high fibre, low fat, no added sugar or salt.

Repositioning. From time to time a company may judge that one of its products is not performing as well as it might. Perhaps the product's original POSITIONING has become unprofitable because of an overcrowded market. By changing some of the product's features, its packaging, its price or advertising appeals, even its DISTRIBUTION CHANNEL, it may be possible to reposition the product so that it becomes more profitable by appealing to a different segment of the market. Both Datsun (Nissan) and Volkswagen have in recent years repositioned their cars from low-priced to mid-priced models. In the 1970s Sherwin Williams (USA) repositioned its traditional housepaint stores to 'decorator centres', broadening the PRODUCT LINE, modernizing the retail outlets and adjusting prices down to be competitive with mass MERCHANDISING stores.

One of the most recent and dramatic repositioning successes was based on a distribution change. The Haynes Company (USA) renamed and repackaged its line of ladies' hosiery and introduced it as a supermarket item. As L'Eggs, it became a runaway success.

Resale price maintenance (RPM). A means by which manufacturers control the retail selling price of their products. Under the terms of the UK Restrictive Trade Practices Act (1956), RPM was not made unlawful, but any company wanting to use it has to defend the practice before the Restrictive Practices Court, and it has proved to be very difficult to make a successful defence. The most notable success, however, was the Net Book Agreement of the Publishers' Association. The Association argued that it was in the public interest to maintain a widespread distribution network and that this could be done only by restricting retail price competition.

In the USA, the Clayton Act (1914) has long been interpreted to mean that RPM constitutes undue restraint of trade and is therefore illegal. (See MANUFACTURER'S RECOMMENDED PRICE.)

Research and development (R&D). The business function responsible for developing new products. In the past, R&D has been dominated by engineering and production-oriented people. The MARKETING CONCEPT, however, which requires that products be created to serve identifiable consumer needs, makes MARKETING RESEARCH an essential part of the R&D process. The British record for INNOVATION is somewhat overshadowed by the failure of many innovations to become economically viable – a situation pointing to product development without reference to market demand.

Research brief. A written statement defining the objectives of a

"Gentlemen, we have to decide whether it's a miracle of spage-age technology or lovingly fashioned by skilled craftsmen."

piece of MARKETING RESEARCH. When a company commissions a research agency to undertake a marketing research survey, it briefs the agency as to what it wants to find out and how much it is prepared to spend. When both company and agency agree that the objectives are both precise and relevant, they are formalized and become the research brief. A good research brief is essential to successful research.

Research Surveys of Great Britain Ltd (RSGB). One of the largest MARKETING RESEARCH companies in the UK. They offer a number of OMNIBUS SURVEYS, run the JICRAR (JOINT INDUSTRY COMMITTEE ON RADIO AUDIENCE RESEARCH) survey, have a product research division and are extensively involved in social research.

Retail life cycle. See WHEEL OF RETAILING.

Retailer. The retailer is at the consumer end of the DISTRIBUTION CHANNEL, providing customers with goods and services, usually from shops. There are nearly two million retailers in the USA and over 400,000 in the UK.

There are many types of retailers: department stores, single or with one or two branch stores; MULTIPLES, chains with shops in many places; limited line and single line stores; SUPERMARKETS; cooperatives, mass merchandisers; SUPERSTORES; even door-to-door sellers are a form of retailing.

Table 16 shows the relative importance of the four major types of retail outlet in the UK in 1978 and 1982.

Table 16   *Retail outlets in the UK*

	Large multiples		Small multiples	
	Number	Sales (£m)	Number	Sales (£m)
1978	63,800	19,500	67,933	6,165
1982	63,200	31,700	76,346	8,812
	One-shop independents		Co-ops	
	Number	Sales (£m)	Number	Sales (£m)
1978	207,900	11,860	10,207	3, 004
1982	203,100	17,270	6,945	4,061

Sales data are exclusive of VAT. Non-registered traders numbered about 35,000 one-shop independents in 1982 with total sales of about £550 million. Mail-order companies are not included; their sales in 1982 were £2131 million (excluding VAT). *Source:* data provided courtesy of Professor John Dawson, Stirling University.

Retailer co-operatives. Retailer co-operation has come about in recent years because independent retailers have had to fight fierce competition from chain stores, particularly in the grocery field. By co-operating with one another on a voluntary basis, they have been able to secure some benefits, such as quantity discounts from manufacturers. Sponsors of co-operation may be the retailers themselves, or the initiative may come from wholesalers.

In the UK, retailer co-operation is dominated by wholesaler sponsorship (see VOLUNTARY CHAINS). In the USA there are examples of co-operation organized by retailers themselves, such as Associated Grocers and True Value (hardware).

Retailer co-operation is quite different from the CO-OPERATIVE MOVEMENT.

Rolling launch. The process of gradually introducing a new product into the market. The first stage might be putting the product through a MARKET TEST. If successful, distribution will be extended, perhaps to another test area, until eventually the whole market will be covered. (See NATIONAL LAUNCH.)

S

Sales agent. See MANUFACTURER'S AGENT.

Sales forecast. An estimate of how much a company hopes to sell to a MARKET, worked out for each PRODUCT. It forms the basis for establishing SALES QUOTAS for salesmen.

Sales forecasting is an exacting skill. It is particularly difficult to estimate sales for a new product, for which no sales experience exists upon which to build the forecast. The forecast may be built upon demand for similar products already in existence or upon the results of a MARKET TEST of the product.

Forecasting for already established products is somewhat easier, but analysing the dynamics of the market, which are constantly changing, still requires considerable skill and insight. Statistical tools such as TIME-SERIES ANALYSIS (using the pattern of historical sales as a basis for forecasting further sales) and multiple regression MODELS (models that identify the factors that cause or influence sales) are employed. Judgemental forecasts (the views of managers, the sales force, industrial goods buyers or distributors) are still very popular.

Sales management. Most marketing organizations employ sales personnel, the sales force as it is often called. The management of this sales force is the responsibility of sales management. The selling function is obviously important – it is, after all, the source of the company's revenue – and sales management is a vital marketing function. In a very large market, as in the USA, there will often be a hierarchy of sales managers, district managers reporting to regional managers who report to a national sales manager or sales vice-president. In the UK regional sales managers (reporting to a sales director) are not uncommon.

Sales promotion. The use of sales incentives designed to produce immediate customer response, such as price reductions, redeemable COUPONS, PREMIUM OFFERS, two for ones or multi-packs, give-aways, competitions. Usually offered at the point of purchase and for a limited period. (See BELOW THE LINE.)

Sales quota. A sales quota specifies the amount that a company expects a salesperson to sell in a year, sometimes quarter by quarter. Sales quotas are based on the company's SALES FORECAST;

*"I'm a little worried about her. Seven years old and still
no interest in bargain offers."*

they may be set higher than the sales forecast, however, in order
to encourage the efforts of the sales force. Salespersons' earnings
are often related to the extent to which they meet or exceed their
quotas.

Sales response function. The relationship between likely sales
volume during a specified period of time and different levels of
marketing support. Other things being equal, the higher the
level of marketing support, particularly ADVERTISING and SALES
PROMOTION and selling support, the more of the product is likely
to be sold, until the point of diminishing returns is reached.
Though it hardly counts as a science, marketing managers do try
to calculate sales response functions, using judgement, statistical
analysis of past sales and marketing expenditures, and occasionally experimentation – perhaps in a TV region where the results
of increasing advertising expenditures can be measured.

Sales revenue. Revenue deriving from sales of a company's products and/or services, often referred to as turnover. Gross profit is equal to sales revenue less cost of sales.

Sales territory. The basic unit of organization of a sales force. Each salesperson will be assigned an exclusive territory in which to sell the company's products. It is the salesperson's responsibility to develop and cultivate contacts in the territory, and to accept credit (or blame) for the sales performance, at least to the extent that the role of PERSONAL SELLING can be differentiated from other elements in the MARKETING MIX. (See SALES MANAGEMENT.)

Samples. Products, sometimes specially packaged, which are given away to consumers, often to induce them to try a new product. They may be delivered to the home, mailed, attached to other products or given away in the retail store. Samples are an effective but potentially expensive way of getting a product into the hands of consumers. Lever Brothers are thought to have placed samples of their new (1978) mouthwash, Signal, in two out of very three homes in America at a cost of $15 million. (See SALES PROMOTION.)

Sampling. Taking a limited number (a sample) from a large group (the population or universe) so that by studying the part something may be learned about the whole. Sampling theory has a very sound statistical basis. It enables the researcher to estimate with reasonable accuracy how representative a sample is likely to be. Generally speaking, the larger the sample the more accurate the result but the greater the cost of the survey, a matter of very important practical concern. With smaller samples, the cost is less but a greater margin of error must be allowed for. Fortunately, most MARKETING RESEARCH projects do not require the very highest degree of accuracy and samples are usually small. Consumer goods research on national samples normally involve 1500–2000 respondents. Minimum samples would be in the order of 300–500 respondents. The UK government's national housing survey includes 100,000 households, an exceptionally large sample.

In survey research 'population' is always defined as the population of interest – all the people who have the characteristics in which the researcher is interested. The population might be all the inhabitants of the country, all telephone owners, all train commuters, all parents of school-age children or all eligible voters.

The selection of people who are to make up the sample may be made in several ways. For purposes requiring the greatest statistical validity, random or probability sampling is used, involving some unbiased means of selection such as drawing names from the telephone book or the electoral role. For many marketing research objectives, however, samples may be chosen more selectively, as in QUOTA SAMPLING and JUDGEMENT SAMPLING (see NON-PROBABILITY SAMPLING).

Scrambled merchandising. A picturesque American term which describes the tendency of retailers to move away from specialized selling into whatever product areas are profitable. Drug stores in the USA and newsagent shops in the UK, for example, usually carry many products other than drugs or newspapers and the variety of merchandise available at supermarkets ranges far beyond food products.

Secondary data. As used in MARKETING RESEARCH, the term applies to all information that may be available to researchers engaged in a specific project which they themselves have not gathered directly by field work for that project. It includes all the data collected and published by government and commercial research firms; data contained in company records; and data previous gathered by researchers. (See PRIMARY DATA.)

Segmentation. See MARKET SEGMENTATION.

Self-liquidating offer. A SALES PROMOTION offer, most easily explained by an example. In order to promote sales, a manufacturer offers customers who buy his product (Product A) at the regular price the chance to buy Product B at a price well below the normal price, usually at least a third less. The customer will have to send the manufacturer some proof of purchase of Product A – a box top, for instance – with his money. The manufacturer will have acquired Product B at low cost: stock-clearance items, possibly, or a quantity purchase directly from another manufacturer. The price paid by customers who take up the offer, though well below retail price, will still be high enough to cover the cost of Product B to the manufacturer; thus the offer which promotes the sales of Product A pays for itself – it is self-liquidating.

Popular items typically offered by manufacturers in this kind of promotion are T-shirts, mugs and kitchen ware.

Self-service. The removal of sales personnel from many shopping places is a development that has moved very fast in the last two decades. Grocery stores pioneered self-service, but the system is now pervasive, in department stores with their central cash desks, in petrol/gas stations and even garage repair shops (USA). It is clearly a marketing response to the cost of labour, and in most cases it appears to be to the satisfaction of customers.

Selling concept. The assumption that salesmen and hard selling are the keys to getting consumers to buy, an approach many companies still use. Those who subscribe to the MARKETING CONCEPT, however, take the view that 'the aim of marketing is to make selling superfluous' (Peter Drucker).

Served market. That part or segment of the total MARKET for which a company provides a product or service – that part of the market which a company serves. (See MARKET SEGMENTATION.)

Services. The marketing of services in contrast to products is the faster-growing segment of economic activity in both the USA and the UK. Services become more important as affluence increases: the demand for banks, stockbrokers, insurance, restaurants, airlines, hotels, museums, theatres, concerts, holidays are all functions of affluence. Growth and competition have encouraged service firms to take an interest in marketing. Airlines, banks and insurance companies led the way, and now marketing has reached most service fields.

Service marketing requires different marketing approaches, because services are fundamentally different from products. Products are not tangible: a pair of pliers can be seen and tested before purchase, but a wedding photograph cannot. They are inseparable from their source: a haircut does not exist apart from the barber. They are perishable: a seat on an airplane unsold at takeoff is a sale lost forever. And they are variable: a weekend in a hotel in London will not be the same as a weekend in a hotel in New York.

Shrinkage. A euphemism for the stock in a retail outlet that disappears without going through the cash register. In other words, it is the stock that is damaged, shoplifted, stolen, or in the case of perishables, left over and either thrown or given away.

"The main problem is, Wilberforce, that we are totally out of touch with what the public wants. Shoplifting figures are down 12% on last year's."

Simulation. An acting out of a marketing situation for test purposes. There are two types of simulation used in MARKETING RESEARCH: computer simulation and laboratory simulation. In computer simulation, data are read into the computer which allow the results of a range of possible actions to be compared. For example, an advertiser might want to test MEDIA expenditure plans. A computer simulation would be able to show the probable results in terms of consumer behaviour of various advertising actions (TV commercials at a variety of times, newspapers advertisements in a variety of papers at different times, etc.).

Laboratory simulation is often used to test BRAND purchasing behaviour, particularly in respect to price. In a simulated store situation (called simulated store technique), a group of shoppers are invited into a room where they are given a sum of money and are asked to spend it on a range of branded products presented to them. After they have completed their purchases, they are suitably diverted while the prices on the products are changed. The shoppers are then given another sum of money to spend and the differences, if any, in their choices are noted.

Skimming. A pricing strategy often used when a new product is introduced into the market. New products tend to be price-inelastic (see PRICE ELASTICITY); in other words, the demand for them is relatively insensitive to their price. The price maker, therefore, sets a high price for the product in the introductory stage of the PRODUCT LIFE CYCLE and attracts a consumer group that values the prestige of owning something new or equates high price with high quality. As the product matures and sales slow down, the price will be lowered to attract new customers into the market. Prices may be reduced several times in the process of skimming, allowing a company to make high revenues from each additional consumer segment.

A skimming strategy can be seen in the marketing of products like cameras, pocket calculators, computers and video recorders.

Smartcard. The French equivalent of EFTPOS (ELECTRONIC FUNDS TRANSFER AT POINT OF SALE): a very clever plastic card that has a tiny micro-processor built into it, giving it processing powers and a memory. The card not only pays its owner's bills (by transferring funds from the bank), but it keeps the account up to date and remembers every transaction. Smartcard, however, is still in the experimental stage.

Social class. See SOCIAL GRADING.

Social grading. A system for classifying social status. The classification system used in the UK was developed for the INSTITUTE OF

PRACTITIONERS IN ADVERTISING by Research Services Ltd and is used for the NATIONAL READERSHIP SURVEY. Details of the system, which is based on the occupation of the head of household, are shown in Table 17.

Table 17 *Social grading (UK)*

Per cent of population 15+	Social grade	Social status	Head of household's occupation
3	A	Upper middle class	Higher managerial, administrative or professional
14	B	Middle class	Intermediate managerial, admin. or professional
22	C1	Lower middle class	Supervisory, clerical, jr managerial, admin., professional
29	C2	Skilled working class	Skill manual workers
18	D	Working class	Semi and unskilled manual workers
14	E	Lowest levels	State pensioners, widows, casual workers

Source: JICNARS National Readership Survey, 1985.

In the USA there is no standard system of social grading. One commonly used, however, (shown in Table 18), is based on behavioural characteristics. Lower middle class, for example, is defined as 'the typical law-abiding, hard-working, church-going American with occupations focussed on non-managerial office work and blue-collar jobs, respectability a key motivation, conformity rather than innovativeness the rule'.

Social grading is considered by many to be a less useful tool for segmenting consumers (see MARKET SEGMENTATION) than systems based on other factors, such as LIFESTYLES or neighbourhoods (see A CLASSIFICATION OF RESIDENTIAL NEIGHBOURHOODS).

Social marketing. Marketing applied to ideas, causes or practices. There is some case for calling it social-cause marketing. Typical examples are anti-smoking campaigns and campaigns encouraging the wearing of seat belts, both trying to change people's

Table 18 *Social grading (USA)*

	Approx. percentage of population
Upper upper class	0.5
Lower upper class	2.5
Upper middle class	12.0
Lower middle class	30.0
Upper lower class	35.0
Lower lower class	20.0

practices. Charities market a cause when they seek donations, and an organization like Friends of the Earth tries to change ideas by marketing concern for the environment.

> Inventors, scientists, engineers and academics in the normal pursuit of scientific knowledge, gave the world in recent times the laser, xerography, instant photography and the transistor. In contrast, worshippers of the marketing concept have bestowed upon mankind such products as new fangled potato chips, feminine hygiene, deodorant and the pet rock . . .
>
> R. H. Hayes & W. J. Abernathy,
> *Harvard Business Review*, July/August 1980

Societal marketing concept. MARKETING which takes into consideration the long-range welfare of society. The widespread acceptance of the MARKETING CONCEPT has not brought to an end the debate about the role of marketing in society. The marketing concept focusses on satisfying individual consumer needs and wants, but there are numerous critics of marketing who point out that there is always a potential conflict between consumers' wants and the long-range interests of society. A classic example is the detergent industry. Detergents have made household laundering very much easier and more efficient, but they have also polluted rivers.

Much of the concern about the anti-social effects of marketing activity has come first from the ecology lobby and latterly from the nutrition lobby, deeply concerned about the dangers to health caused by modern convenience foods. The societal marketing concept recognizes the legitimacy of many of these concerns. It requires companies to recognize that they must bring three interests into balance – those of the consumer, those of the company, and those of society as a whole – and that failure to do so will in the long run produce problems for all three.

Solus sites. Retail outlets that carry the PRODUCT LINE of one company only, such as petrol/gas stations. The term 'solus user' refers to consumers who use only one brand – the person who drinks only Smirnoff or drives only Jaguars.

Specialist research. Some MARKETING RESEARCH agencies gather specialized data. A. C. NIELSEN, for example, concentrates on retail audits, but specialist research services exist for a wide range of subjects, such as agriculture, children, MEDIA, motoring, pharmaceuticals, packaging and tourism. In the UK, details of specialist research services are provided in the MARKET RESEARCH SOCIETY's *Organizations Providing Market Research Services in Great Britain.* (See OFF-THE-PEG RESEARCH.)

Spiffs. See PUSH MONEY.

Sponsorship. The subsidizing of an event, usually sporting or artistic, by a company for advertising purposes. Events receiving wide MEDIA coverage bring the company name (or one of its products) to the attention of millions of viewers and associate it with a pleasurable experience. In the UK, sports sponsorship has grown from a £35 million business in 1980 to over £100 million in 1983, representing approximately 90 per cent of all UK sponsorships.

Sponsorship of the arts, though a poor relation of sports sponsorship, is also growing. It is one way a company can promote its CORPORATE IMAGE, especially favoured by companies engaged in businesses not generally associated with culture. Texaco, for example, has sponsored Saturday afternoon broadcasts of the Metropolitan Opera for many decades, and Shell is known for its sponsorship of British art and artists.

Sponsorship is a way to avoid certain restrictions imposed by advertising codes of practice. Whisky cannot be advertised on British television, but Bells whisky was the prominent sponsor of a recently televised golf tournament. Cigarette manufacturers,

"I see the Hitachi deal fell through."

likewise barred from direct TV advertising, sponsor many sporting events – motor racing (Marlboro), tennis (Virginia Slims), cricket (Benson & Hedges).

Standard Industrial Classification (SIC). The closest thing we have to a classification of goods sytem in marketing. There is a SIC scheme in both the UK and the USA, and though not identical, they are very similar, both based on a decimal code. For example, in the USA a pair of pliers would be coded SIC 342311. The first two digits identify the basic industry: the numbers from 19 to 39 indicate manufactured goods, the number 34 specifying fabricated metal products. The rest of the digits are as follows:

3rd	Industry group	2 = cutlery, handtools, hardware
4th	Specific industry	3 = hand and edge tools
5th	Product class	1 = mechanics hand service tools
6th	Product	1 = pliers

All government statistics relating to industrial production in both countries are published under SIC codes and are therefore a valuable SECONDARY DATA source for marketing researchers.

Stars. Brands with high markets shares in high growth markets. They are potentially very profitable but need strong investment support to maintain their market shares until their markets mature. (See GROWTH/SHARE MATRIX.)

Sterling distribution. A colloquial British term, much loved by brand managers, referring to the way a manufacturer may try to distribute his products to retail outlets. If there are 1000 outlets that might handle the manufacturer's products, and 250 of them account for 50 per cent of all the money spent by customers in the thousand outlets, the manufacturer would achieve 50 per cent sterling distribution if he managed to have his products stocked by those 250 outlets. Sterling, of course, refers to British currency.

Stock control. The management of the inventory of retail and wholesale outlets, a very exacting task. Inventory is capital that is tied up; only when it is sold does it produce cash and profits. Skilful stock control will keep inventory levels high enough to ensure that goods are available when customers want them, but not so high that too much of the company's capital is invested unproductively in unsold goods. For a retailer stock turn-around (keeping stock moving) is a major factor in determining profitability, and failure to manage stock correctly (maintain sufficient inventory) can result in 'stock outs', which mean frustrated or even lost customers.

Store audits. A measurement of what is being purchased in shops. Store or retail audits are routinely made by retail store management, but they are also carried out by major research suppliers, like A. C. NIELSEN, who offer the data for sale. Such information is of great interest to marketing and brand managers as a measure of the performance of their products (see BRAND MANAGEMENT).

Store image. No British shopper would deny that Harrods has a different character from Boots, just as American shoppers recognize the difference between Saks Fifth Avenue and J. C. Penney's. A store's image depends on factors such as decor, layout, the type of merchandise it carries, the kind of service it offers, all of which serve to position the store for a target market.

Storyboard. Device which shows the elements of a TELEVISION

COMMERCIAL. The board is composed of a series of frames carrying in sketch or cartoon form the idea development of the commercial. Storyboards are an essential tool in the creative departments of ADVERTISING AGENCIES and may also be used in PRE-TESTING advertisements.

Strategic business unit (SBO). An autonomous division within a company, usually a large multi-product company, responsible for planning the marketing of one of the company's major product ranges. Thus General Foods has six SBUs: breakfast foods, beverages, main meal products, coffee, desserts and pet foods.

From the point of view of top management, SBUs represent the company's portfolio of product offerings and are the units of analysis in PORTFOLIO ANALYSIS; planning at corporate level sets long-range objectives and allocates resources for individual SBUs. Within the SBU, managers are responsible for developing their own strategies or long-term plans for their product or mix of products, in line with the corporate objectives.

SBUs are accountable to top management but independent of each other. They may serve different markets, grow at different rates, have different competitors and different objectives: product reduction, for example, might be the objective of one SBU while the addition of a new product might be the goal of another.

SBUs are basically strategic planning units. Their advantage to a company is that they tend to focus managers' minds on long-range profitability rather than short-term profits. (See PLANNING.)

Strategic planning. See PLANNING.

Structured interview. A type of interview used in MARKETING RESEARCH in which the interviewer asks the questions exactly as they appear on the QUESTIONNAIRE, adding nothing nor explaining anything to the respondent. The respondent may answer only 'yes', 'no' or 'don't know'. This impersonal technique produces data that can be quickly and easily tabulated, but it places a heavy burden on the designer of the questionnaire. Inaccurate data resulting from badly constructed questions will not be detected and will affect the validity of the research.

Structured interviews are used when it is the measurability of the data that is of importance to the research, questions of 'how many' or 'how much' (see QUANTITATIVE RESEARCH).

The semi-structured interview combines features of the structured interview and GROUP DISCUSSION. Interviewers must use the wording of the questionnaire, but the questionnaire uses questions which allow the respondent to answer freely, e.g. 'What are the factors important to you?' (see OPEN-ENDED QUESTION). This type of interview produces fuller information but in a form more difficult to tabulate and analyse.

Supermarket. A large, high-volume, SELF-SERVICE store. It is usually operated on a low-margin, high-turnover (volume) basis, and has come to dominate the grocery trade. It is making substantial inroads into many other product fields as well, including pharmaceuticals, home improvements (DIY), and clothing.

It is generally agreed that the supermarket idea was born in the USA. John Hart Ford introduced cash-and-carry grocery retailing when he started the Great Atlantic and Pacific Tea Company (the A & P) food stores in 1912. Clarence Saunders opened his Piggly-Wiggly stores in the USA in 1916 in which self-service and customer checkouts were pioneered.

Supermarkets are distinguished from SUPERSTORES and HYPER-MARKETS by their smaller size (less than 25,000 square feet) and their greater concentration on food products.

Supersites. See POSTERS.

Superstores. Large modern stores which are growing in importance in the UK. They can be technically defined as single-storey structures of from 25,000 to 49,000 square feet located next to a

Table 19 *Number of superstores, by type, from 1981 to 1983*

	1981	1982	1983
Total superstores	297	333	356
Cooperatives	44	49	64
Multiples, including independents	253	284	292

Source: A. C. Nielsen Co., Ltd.

free car park big enough to hold at least 250 cars. They sell food stuffs predominantly, but up to 30 per cent of their sales area may be devoted to non-food items, primarily DIY, hardware and motor-car accessories. Popularly, they are synonymous with HYPERMARKETS, although technically hypermarkets are bigger (50,000 square feet and up) and can sell proportionately more non-food products. (See Table 19.)

SWOT analysis. In the PLANNING proces, before marketing objectives and strategies are defined, it is important for marketing managers to assess the company's Strengths and Weaknesses and the Opportunities and Threats facing it. SWOT is the name given to such an analysis (made up from the initial letters).

Internal factors are examined in order to identify strengths and weaknesses. A company might identify an excellent service network, a widespread distribution system, or experience in international marketing as strengths that could be exploited in marketing strategies. Poor cash flow or an over-extended PRODUCT MIX might be seen as weaknesses to be corrected.

Opportunities and threats, on the other hand, are external

factors. Careful scanning of the marketing environment might reveal opportunities a company could exploit arising from new technological developments, an unmet consumer need, or some vulnerability in the competition. Threats might be perceived in changing consumer buying behaviour, government legislation or some international situation.

In recent planning practice, this analysis has demonstrated its value in setting sound and realistic objectives and strategies.

Symbols. A term used in the UK to describe VOLUNTARY CHAIN members, such as Spar, Mace or VG. It derives from the prominence of the voluntary group's indentifying mark – its PRIVATE LABEL – used on much of the merchandise carried in their stores.

Syndicated research. Large-scale MARKETING RESEARCH undertaken by marketing research firms and offered for sale. It is not research undertaken for a client. A. C. NIELSEN's retail auditing is an example of syndicated research. Some agencies use DIARY PANELS to record family purchases and analyse changes in LIFESTYLE; others evaluate print and TELEVISION ADVERTISING and MEDIA exposure.

Systems selling. Selling a total system rather than an individual product. In the information-processing field, for example, it is clearly to the advantage of a company such as IBM to sell a complete operating system (hardware, software, peripherals). Indeed systems selling starts with the buyer's requirements and designs a system to meet them. A firm manufacturing robotic equipment would try to persuade a customer that his complete production line should be analysed for a changeover to robotics. A hospital equipment supplier would try to sell a fully equipped operating theatre rather than separate components. From the buyer's point of view, although systems buying might cost more in the short term, it is probable that a complete and compatible system will operate more efficiently than would components purchased separately from different suppliers over a longer period of time.

T

Tachistoscope. A MARKETING RESEARCH device for measuring the extent to which a consumer registers the BRAND and other relevant information displayed on a package. The tachistoscope ('swiftest look') shows pictures of a package for various time periods, enabling researches to test the effectiveness of design, colour, brand name, for instance, before the package is sent out to take its place on the crowded shelves of the retail outlet.

Target Group Index (TGI). An example of SYNDICATED RESEARCH undertaken on a continuous basis by the British Market Research Bureau. The Index is an annual report based on self-completion QUESTIONNAIRES (no interviewer present) from a RANDOM SAMPLING of 24,000 respondents on their use of hundreds of PRODUCTS and thousands of BRANDS.

Target marketing. The selection of one or more segments of the market for special attention by a company. As consumers become more affluent and more discerning, it becomes more difficult to market products that satisfy everyone. Most market-oriented companies, therefore, offer products aimed at specific groups of consumers. (See MARKET SEGMENTATION.)

Tariff. A tax on imported goods. Few governments resist the temptation to tax imports. The tax is usually raised against the declared value of the imported goods, known as an *ad valorem* duty. The impact on free-world trade of tariff barriers has been greatly ameliorated by the most favoured nation principle used by GATT (GENERAL AGREEMENT ON TARIFFS AND TRADE) to bring about tariff reductions among its member nations.

Telephone research. As telephone ownership increases (it is almost universal in the USA) telephone research grows in popularity among marketing researchers. It is more economical than personal interviewing, and most respondents appear to be willing to talk over the phone, perhaps more willing than they would be in a personal interview.

Telephone interviewing was developed as a research method in industrial market research. It has always been easier to contact busy executives by phone.

Until telephone ownership is universal in the UK, telephone

research will have its limitations because ownership will be biased in favour of middle-class consumers.

COMPUTER–ASSISTED TELEPHONE INTERVIEWING (CATI) has enabled researchers to interview more effectively and to speed up data analysis.

Telephone selling. In the USA, telephone selling is a common form of sales prospecting and also a means for making sales presentations. In industrial marketing it has been in use for some time. The telephone reduces wasted sales calls and visits and helps to identify good prospects for a follow-up sales visit. The consumer may on occasion regard it as an invasion of privacy. (See DIRECT MARKETING.)

Tele-selling. The prospect of purchasing goods from the convenience of one's own home is quite close. The information revolution has already brought data service into the living room – Prestel and Teletext in the UK, for example, and VIDEOTEXT in the USA. The next step is to bring a catalogue display onto the domestic television screen. Using an interactive data link (as Prestel and Videotext can already do) consumers will be able to order goods directly – and have their bank accounts debited directly as well!

Television commercials. Better than most TV programmes? Bane of television viewing? Useful breaks for tea or coffee? Whether we like them or not, television commercials have become an integral part of our viewing lives, and judging from the amount marketers spend on television ADVERTISING, they would appear to be powerful persuaders. 23 per cent of all American advertising expenditure went on television in 1984, and in the UK, 30 per cent. See ADVERTISING EXPENDITURE USA and ADVERTISING EXPENDITURE UK.

Television ratings (TVRs). Measures of television programme popularity based on survey research. Sophisticated equipment is attached to sets in selected homes (a QUOTA SAMPLE) to record which channel the set is tuned to. DIARY PANELS are used to determine how many people are watching the set. Ratings are calculated as a minute-by-minute programme audience and expressed as a percentage of total households which can receive TV.

Advertisers measure the coverage of their advertising campaigns in TVRs, the percentage of a target audience (housewives, teenagers, men) having the television on during the spot (commercial).

Audience research is undertaken in the USA by A. C. NIELSEN and in the UK by the BROADCASTERS AUDIENCE RESEARCH BOARD (BARB).

Tendering. Making a bid for a contract, a practice used in marketing to governments and other organizations. Tendering gives all suppliers a fair and equal chance of obtaining the business contract. Without tendering, subjective factors, friendship, political influence, etc., might influence the selection of a contractor. Tenders are often invited on a sealed-bid basis. The bidder quoting the lowest price is normally awarded the contract.

Tender notices are widely publicized and in the case of international tendering are advertised in countries thought capable of bidding for the contract.

Tendering is used for hospital, airport, university construction, for bridge-building projects, and for much defence work, as well as for more modest contracts such as supplying food to a prison or a military base.

In the USA the term 'competitive bidding' is used.

Test market. See MARKET TEST.

Threshold effect. The point at which ADVERTISING begins to be effective. Advertising costs money. How much to spend on advertising is one of the most difficult decisions marketing managers have to make. It is not easy to measure the effectiveness of advertising because we know its effects last a long time. Products sold this week in the supermarket may be sold because of the accumulated effects of advertising over several years. Lord Lever said that he knew his company was wasting half the money they spent on advertising, but the trouble was that nobody could tell him which half! The problem with advertising is that quite a lot of money has to be spent on it before it produces any effect. This may not be the case with an insertion in the classified section of a local newspaper – that often works very quickly and effectively – but in large-scale marketing, when a company is selling its PRODUCT LINE to a national market, it takes a considerable investment for its advertising even to begin to be noticed in the midst of so much advertising already in existence.

The threshold effect, therefore, is important because it sets the minimum limit on an advertising budget. Unless advertising expenditure for a brand reaches a certain level, it will be money wasted.

Time-series analysis. A technique used in sales forecasting. Historical sales data are analyzed in order to understand the reasons for fluctuations over time. The causal relations thus uncovered can then be used to forecast future sales. The major components of a time series are trend, cycle and seasonal events. Historical data decomposed in this way often provide valuable insights into sales behaviour, but there is, of course, no guarantee that all components will behave in the same way in the future. (See SALES FORECAST.)

Trade discount. The means by which members of the DISTRIBU-TION CHANNEL ('the trade') are paid for the services they perform. Manufacturers offer discounts on their list prices to wholesalers, who in turn discount their prices to retailers. Such discounts, because they are given for functions performed, are called functional discounts. Trade discounts may also be related to the speed at which the goods are expected to sell.

In addition to trade discounts, manufacturers frequently offer QUANTITY DISCOUNTS to wholesalers. It is also normal to offer discounts for prompt payments of accounts, called cash discounts. A cash discount might be expressed as '3/14 net 28', which means the buyer (wholesaler or retailer) will be given a three per cent discount if he pays within 14 days and that the bill must be settled within 28 days.

Trade-in allowance. A price reduction given for a used good when similar goods are purchased new. It is an indirect form of price cutting. In car retailing, prices advertised by dealers may appear to be uniform. Price competition takes place, however, when the trade-in allowance on the old car is being negotiated. In the case of DURABLE GOODS (stoves/cookers, refrigerators, etc.), trade-in allowances are often nominal and are frequently advertised.

Trade mark. A legal term, covering words, symbols or marks that have been legally registered by a company, a BRAND name or CORPORATE LOGO must be registered for a company to have the proprietary right to use it.

Trade marketing. The focussing of marketing efforts by manufacturers on the DISTRIBUTION CHANNEL ('the trade'), primarily on large retail chains. Marketing is normally defined in terms of a firm's relationship with consumers. The growth in the power of the large retail CHAIN STORE, however, has meant that it may no longer be enough to promote products only to consumers (see PUSH vs PULL STRATEGY); manufacturers may also have to direct their marketing efforts towards powerful retailers in order to secure distribution for their products at acceptable TRADE DISCOUNTS. (See DISTRIBUTION and NATIONAL ACCOUNT MANAGEMENT.)

Trade-off analysis. See CONJOINT ANALYSIS.

Trading stamps. Free stamps given by retailers against the value of purchases made and usually redeemable for catalogue merchandise or cash. Retailers sometimes have their own stamps (the Co-operative retail stores in the UK), or they purchase them from trading-stamp companies (S & H Green Stamps in the USA). The use of trading stamps in grocery retailing was very common in the 1960s, but any COMPETITIVE ADVANTAGE they represented for a retailer disappeared when every other retailer offered similar stamps.

Trading up. Marketing slang for moving UP MARKET.

Transactions. EXCHANGE is a core element in marketing. If two parties are engaged in exchange and reach an agreement, a transaction takes place. Transactions normally involve money. I pay a sum of money to a retailer and he allows me to take away the product(s) I want. A transaction can occur without money exchanging hands. Indeed, most primitive types of marketing activity involved barter transaction – a tribal villager exchanging a bowl of wheat for his neighbour's sheepskin. (See COUNTER TRADING.)

Turnkey operations. Large capital investment projects, usually overseas, carried out by a contractor who is given total responsibility for the design and construction of the project and who, on completion, will turn it over to the owners. Turnkey operations require special marketing skills and strategies. For example, special profit management skills are needed right from the beginning to anticipate the buyer's needs and prepare the contract bid.

In the Middle East in recent years, universities, hospitals, port facilities and chemical plants have been built largely by overseas contractors.

U

Undifferentiated marketing. Marketing a product aimed at the widest possible market, appealing to needs that unite rather than divide consumers. For many years the Coca Cola Company produced only one product in one kind of container, and became very rich in the process. Henry Ford revolutionized automobile production when he mass-produced the Model T for an undifferentiated market: one model for everybody in any colour as long as it was black.

Today undifferentiated marketing has largely given way to the concept and practice of MARKET SEGMENTATION. Coca Cola now produces Classic Coke, New Coke, Cherry Coke, Diet Coke, Fanta and Sprite – in large bottles, small bottles, glass bottles, plastic bottles and cans. Every motor-car manufacturer, including Ford, now offers a wide range of models and options to suit many different tastes and requirements.

Unique selling proposition (USP). The concept, less popular today than it used to be, that a product should have some unique feature about it, able to be communicated to consumers through advertising, that would differentiate it from its competitors. A continuous stream of products with unique features important to consumers, however, is in practice hard to produce, and USP has given ground to newer ideas of POSITIONING less tied to actual product features.

Unit pricing. A form of pricing used by retailers to enable shoppers to make price comparisons between products. In the USA and to a lesser extent in the UK, large retailers, particularly SUPERMARKET chains, show the price per unit of a PRODUCT in addition to its total price. For example, a grocer might carry four BRANDS of instant coffee, each brand available in three sizes. Each size of each brand will, of course, be marked with a selling price. In addition, however, the price of a unit, say two ounces, of each size of each brand will also be displayed. A four-ounce jar of Brand A might cost 50 pence/cents per unit while an eight-ounce jar of the same brand might cost 47 pence/cents per unit and the one-pound jar 42 pence/cents – and so on for Brands B, C and D. The shopper, therefore, can see at a glance which size jar of which brand is the most economical buy.

Universal product coding (UPC). See BAR CODE.

Up market. A popular term which, with its counterpart 'down market', refers to the structure of a MARKET, visualized as having a top and a bottom and a way to move up and down. Exactly what is meant by the terms depends on how they are applied, as Table 20 shows.

Table 20   *Up and down market*

	Up market	Down market
Class	upper class	lower class
Price	expensive	cheap
Style	exclusive	mass
Quality	high	low
Features	luxury	basic

Marketers use the term chiefly in respect to product POSITIONING and REPOSITIONING. Products may be moved up or down market by changing some element of the MARKETING MIX. Going up market might involve increasing the quality of a product or limiting its distribution to exclusive speciality shops. Removing personal service and luxury fittings from a store or lowering a product's price are ways of going down market.

Upscale. An American term for UP MARKET.

V

Value analysis. A technique a company may use of searching for ways to reduce costs without sacrificing its products' market appeal. Marketing managers and production and design engineers, for example, get together to discuss ways the costs of producing a product might be cut. The ideas thus generated are ranked according to their cost-saving potential and analyzed for feasibility. Any proposed change is checked against consumer perceptions of the product's value.

Value analysis can be applied to new product ideas at the design stage, as well as to existing products.

Van tests. A MARKETING RESEARCH technique in which a mobile van or truck is moved into a convenient place, a supermarket parking lot/car park for example, and used to conduct on the spot product research. (See HALL TESTS.)

Vertical integration. If a manufacturing company acquires its sources of supply, or if it integrates forward to acquire wholesalers, or if it goes into retailing, we observe vertical integration taking place. For example, Bata manufactures shoes and sells through its own retail outlets, as do Clarks and K Shoes in the UK, and Genesco and Florsheim in the USA. The Co-operative Society owns manufacturing plants, though it also buys from other sources. Control over sources of supply or control of DISTRIBUTION are the benefits of vertical integration.

Videotext. A two-way TV cable system in the USA enabling a television viewer to access information from a data base in a central computer and to transmit information back. Videotext can therefore be used for survey research, for opinion polling, and for ordering from a store or a catalogue displayed on the TV screen. It makes TELE-SELLING possible. In the UK, cable is still in its infancy and interactive systems such as Prestel operate over telephone lines. (See DIRECT MARKETING.)

Village store. Represents all that is good, humane and inefficient in retailing. Most of us carry an idealized picture of what shopping used to be like before the decline of the friendly neighbourhood grocer. In reality, given the choice, most people prefer the new ways in shopping to the old. (See RETAILERS.)

Voluntary chains. The growth of grocery chains (see GROCERY MARKET SHARES) has created great problems for independent grocers. Without the buying power of the chain store, they are placed at a disadvantage in terms of price. In many cases they offset this disadvantage by providing convenience in terms of location or opening hours, but independent grocery retailers have been declining in number on both sides of the Atlantic. The voluntary chain movement has been one development that has saved some from extinction. Voluntary chains are organized by wholesalers; they sign up independent retailers who agree to buy from them. By combining the buying power of many independents, the wholesaler acquires buying power with his suppliers. In the UK, Spar, VG and Mace are successful voluntary chains (SYMBOLS), so successful that many products now appear as DEALER BRANDS bearing the name of the voluntary chain. IGA (Independent Grocers Alliance) and Super Value are well-known grocery retailers in the USA as is Western Auto, an automobile accessories voluntary chain.

W

Warranty. A warranty (USA), often called a guarantee in the UK, explains what the seller promises about his product. The Magnuson–Moss Act (USA 1975) states that a manufacturer must produce a clearly written statement about what he promises, that a warranty must be neither unfair nor deceptive, and that it must be clear whether it is a limited or a full warranty.

In the UK, there is no equivalent law covering manufacturers' guarantees, and the obligations of manufacturers in respect to warranties are unclear. Most firms limit the promise they make (limited warranty), often to defects of material or workmanship and usually to a period of a year or less, but conditions are sometimes attached. Retailers, on the other hand, have a legal obligation to provide customers with goods of merchantable quality (see *CAVEAT EMPTOR*).

In marketing practice, guarantees are part of product policy, being seen by customers as an important part of the product they buy. Recently, many durable goods have begun to appear with parts guaranteed for five years and labour for one. The motor-car industry has used guarantees for several years to promote sales, and as a result of competition between manufacturers, new car buyers may be offered free servicing for a period of more than a year and for several thousand miles.

Wheel of retailing. An American theory of retailing based on the fact that retailing is constantly changing. Even over a short period of time it is possible to observe this happening on every high street or in every shopping centre: some retail shops are opening and others are closing. The 'wheel of retailing' theory states that most new retailers start as low-status, low-margin, low-priced operators, and as they prosper they move UP MARKET, leaving opportunities for new entrants. The theory has some explanatory value. Many DISCOUNT STORES started after World War II in the way described by the theory. Some, as they prospered, moved up market into more expensive locations and became as a result higher-status, higher-priced operators.

It can be argued that retailing provides a good example of the life-cycle theory at work (see PRODUCT LIFE CYCLE): department stores, since they first appeared around 1850, have reached maturity and (some would say) gone into decline. Supermarkets have had a shorter life cycle, reaching maturity in about 30 years.

Fast-food outlets appeared only about 15 years ago (the fish and chip shop notwithstanding) and are probably still in the growth stage.

Which? The monthly magazine published by Consumers' Association of the UK. It contains reports on tests made on a wide variety of products and services by the Association in their testing laboratories or the results of MARKETING RESEARCH carried out among members of the Association. (See CONSUMER REPORTS.)

White goods. Washing machines, refrigerators, deep-freezes and stoves (cookers). The term derives from the fact that at one time these DURABLE GOODS were always covered in white enamel paint.

Wholesaling. Wholesalers are intermediary establishments, linking manufacturers and retailers. Full service wholesalers used to dominate wholesaling in both the USA and UK, providing warehousing, a sales force, delivery service, credit, market research, and merchandising and reordering help for retailers, but competitive pressures have reduced their importance. In some cases manufacturers themselves have taken over the wholesaling function, using DISTRIBUTION CENTRES to supply retail outlets. In other cases wholesalers have successfully limited the services they offer to retailers (see CASH AND CARRY WHOLESALING and RACK JOBBERS). Some full service wholesalers have been successful by setting up chains of independent retailers (see VOLUNTARY CHAINS). (See DISTRIBUTION.)

> Don't tell my Mother I'm in Advertising. She thinks I'm a Pianist in a Brothel.
>
> Title of a book by Jacques Sequela,
> campaign adviser to President Mitterrand

Word-of-mouth advertising. It is every marketer's dream to have a product so satisfactory to those who purchase it that they immediately tell their friends and neighbours about it. Word-of-mouth advertising is very powerful, as demonstrated recently by the rapid spread of the game Trivial Pursuit across the USA and the UK in advance of MEDIA advertising.

Z

Zero rated. A term meaningful only to those who live in the land of VAT (value added tax), a form of direct tax in use in the UK and other countries of the European Economic Community. Certain goods – food, books and children's clothing, for example – are not currently subject to value added tax and are said to be zero rated.